Dear HP,
Happy Spring!
All my love
"M"

irresistible

2006

First published in Great Britain in 2005 by Cassell Illustrated,
a division of Octopus Publishing Group Limited
2–4 Heron Quays, London E14 4JP

Distributed in the United States of America by
Sterling Publishing Co., Inc.,
387 Park Avenue South, New York, NY 10016-8810

A CIP catalogue record for this book is available
from the British Library.

ISBN 1 84403 346 5
EAN   9781844033461

Photographs by Jan Baldwin
Styling by Leslie Dilcock
Home Economist Pippa Cuthbert
Design by Martin Lovelock
Art Direction by Jo Knowles
Publishing Manager Anna Cheifetz

Printed in China

ACKNOWLEDGEMENTS

I've always wanted to do an Oscars-style dramatic thank you speech, but I'll promise to keep it short and sweet! Firstly I'd like to thank my Mother, Christiana. Not only for helping me so much with the book at all hours of the night and day. But also for bringing me up single-handedly and being my inspiration and drive behind my career, past, present and future. Thank you to my stepfather, John for being a real father to me. Thank you to my amazing grandparents for nurturing the chef inside me from an early age! And of course love to my little brother (who once was a pain in the arse, but is now shaping up well!). On the business side of things, Tony Fitzpatrick, Anne Kibel and Murray Harkin from TFA, you were the first to believe in me and you got me the book deal – brilliant! Thank you to everyone at Cassells, you all did an excellent job and had to put up with the trials of a first-time author! Thank you to everyone involved with the layout, photos, and styling. You all made my food look rather good! Big thanks to Matthew Vaughn and Claudia Schiffer (Mr and Mrs De Vere Drummond). Such a lovely couple to work for and now such a beautiful family with the addition of Casper and Clementine I really enjoyed my work through that time. That also applies to everyone I've worked with over the years. I've been privileged to work with some of the best in the industry. Last, but certainly not least, thank you to all my wonderful friends, especially Simon who gave me so much love. You all know who you are and you've all been there through thick and thin (a lot of alcohol may have been involved, but I'm of course completely reformed now! Ahem...) Thank you everyone, Big kiss!

irresistible

BEAUTIFUL FOOD • BEAUTIFUL BODY

SOPHIE MICHELL

CASSELL ILLUSTRATED

contents

introduction

This book is not about dieting, it's about using beautiful food to create a beautiful body. You are what you eat, so making a few simple changes to your eating habits can make a big difference to your life. It's not about what you can't eat, it's about all the wonderful foods you can eat! It's not a quick fix but a healthier way of eating.

Chefs obviously love food – what drove me to become a chef was the thought of surrounding myself with fantastic food every day. Which was great...and while I told myself, 'Never trust a skinny chef,' and 'I know I'm overweight, but food is my life and job,'...deep down I wasn't happy with my ever-expanding waistline. At twenty you should be at your optimum fitness. Instead, I felt tired and lethargic. I'd suffered from chronic fatigue syndrome since the age of fourteen and was feeling very ill again. But I couldn't afford to let it affect my work. After seeing several doctors, I was advised to eliminate wheat, sugar and coffee from my diet and this got me thinking more carefully about what I was eating. I scanned the diet books on the market, but they all left me feeling worse. They were all based on deprivation – YUK! A chef deprived of food is not a pretty sight! So, I devised a way to eat high-quality, restaurant-standard food, that would leave me feeling healthy and trim. I'm not a scientist or a doctor, so the principles are very simple.

In our diet we have 'good' carbs (complex carbohydrates) and 'bad' carbs (refined carbohydrates). Good carbs are those found in fruit and vegetables, and also in wholegrain carbohydrates, such as wholemeal pasta, wholemeal flour, brown rice, rye breads, granary breads and wild rice. Bad carbs are what we usually consume. These include white refined flour, white rice, white bread, white pasta and sugar. Bad carbs release sugar into the bloodstream very quickly. This gives us an instant energy rush, only to bring us crashing down after a couple of hours. This is why they don't sustain you and quickly leave you feeling hungry and tired. Once your body is used to this cycle it can be difficult to retrain it. When my doctor told me to give up sugar, I thought it would be easy. I was wrong; cutting it out made me feel really ill – my body was completely addicted to it! Being trapped in the sugar-addiction cycle can affect your temperament (causing mood swings), your concentration levels and, of course, leave you feeling exhausted and depressed. Good carbs, however, release energy slowly into our bloodstream. This means that they sustain you for longer, which, in turn, means you eat less and don't have fluctuations in energy. Good carbs are essential.

I also don't believe in cutting fat out of my eating plan. Your body needs fat. It makes food taste better, it sends signals to your brain that you're full, and it protects your immune system. Without fat we wouldn't be able to absorb vitamins A, D, E and K. Although some fats have been shown to increase the risk of heart disease, other types can reduce it. Studies have shown that extremely low-fat diets may raise levels of bad cholesterol (low-density lipoprotein), while lowering good cholesterol (high-density lipoprotein). Omega-3 fatty acids also fall into this good-fat bracket. They are found in oily fish such as tuna, salmon and sardines. Omega-3 oils are especially good for your hair and skin. The only fats we really shouldn't include in our diet are trans-fatty acids. These are man-made fats found in processed foods and nasties like margarine.

So now to the book. *Irresistible* is based on not mixing proteins and carbohydrates at each meal. You can have a protein or a complex-carb breakfast. I suggest a protein lunch (although there is a complex-carb chapter if you feel the need). And a protein-based dinner. When I say protein-based, I mean that the dish has a high level of protein, but also has the natural carbs found in vegetables. Now for desserts. A question I often hear when serving desserts is, 'Is it a healthy dessert?' I have to say, there's no such thing as a healthy dessert. If it's sweet, it's got sugar in it (natural or not), and that makes it unhealthy. One of the most common mistakes people make is to see a 'low- fat' or 'diet' dessert, think that's great and then eat twice as much as normal. 'Low-fat' usually means it's still packed full of sugar, and often chemicals and stabilisers too. I always say that if you don't recognise most of the ingredients on the back of a packet, don't eat it. We wouldn't take a tablet without knowing what's in it, so why eat a dish made from unknown chemicals? My philosophy is, we're all human and when you've done a month without refined carbs and sugars, you can certainly treat yourself to a small amount of home-made dessert now and again – it's much better for you than shop-bought pap and more satisfying as well. Remember, it's all about balance and enjoying natural food for what it is, so get cooking!

Sophie Michell

a breakfast boost

In my family, having a proper cooked breakfast is
paramount – to the point of obsession. This tradition
has been handed down to me through the generations.
When my mother was a child, she and my great-grandfather
used to get up at dawn in the beautiful Cheshire/Welsh
border country and go out to pick fresh mushrooms from
the fields. Then they went back and fried them up with
bacon from my great-grandfather's own home-reared pigs.
Good, traditional, English breakfast food.

top breakfast tips

So now breakfast is my favourite meal and I love getting my tastebuds going with different flavours. I've included a lot of colourful dishes in this chapter, but I'll admit that most mornings time can be too limited for me to be cooking very much. So I've given you a few ideas to help with brekky on-the-run.

- Never miss breakfast. I cannot stress how important for weight management this is. It's an easy meal to miss, yet it has a massive effect on your body's metabolism. Eat something as soon as you can after waking up. This will literally kick-start your metabolism. Without it, your body just won't start processing and burning fat.

- If choosing carbohydrates, always stick to complex carbs. These are wholegrain products such as granary and rye breads, wholegrain cereals, and so on.

- If choosing a protein breakfast, go for good-quality produce: for example, nitrate-free organic bacon and free-range eggs.

- Try to avoid piling on the sugary jams and syrups. Opt for low-sugar jams and spreads instead.

- In the Western world, our main breakfast staples are often refined carbohydrates (such as toast, jam) and caffeine (tea, coffee). Typically, these are the worst things you can eat. They give you a quick boost which makes you wake up and run, but by eleven o' clock you crash back down and start feeling tired, lethargic and hungry. Hence the need for elevenses which usually consists of nice (but unhealthy), sugary foods. So here are some quick, easy breakfast fixes which are much more healthy and sustaining, for those mornings when you are short of time:

- Low-fat yoghurt and fruit
- Wholegrain toast and low-sugar jam
- Sliced avocado on toasted rye bread
- Wholegrain cereals with soya or semi-skimmed milk
- Hard- or soft-boiled eggs

You can enjoy some of the following breakfast recipes for lazy weekends or power-breakfast mornings.

slow-roasted tomatoes, crispy bacon and poached eggs

A high-protein breakfast will sustain you well into lunchtime – and this, for me, is the ultimate 'fry-up'. I used to be put off by the heavy feeling that many cooked breakfasts leave behind, but this one should leave you full of energy and raring to go. Try to use good, organic bacon and free-range eggs: apart from anything else, the flavour is so much better.

SERVES 4

8 rashers smoked or non-smoked streaky bacon, preferably organic
4 cherry tomatoes
splash of olive oil
salt and freshly ground black pepper
4–8 eggs, depending on the size of your appetite

Preheat the grill to high, then put the bacon on a baking sheet and grill for a couple of minutes, just to start it cooking. Add the whole tomatoes to the bacon tray, sprinkle with olive oil and season with salt and pepper to taste. Continue grilling the bacon until it is really crispy and the tomatoes are nearly bursting. This should take about 8 minutes.

While the bacon and tomatoes are cooking, poach the eggs (see page 187). Serve the poached eggs with the bacon and tomatoes. Enjoy!

more ideas

- Grilled tomatoes are also delicious sprinkled with dried oregano (Greek-style) or with shredded, fresh basil.

- Serve this breakfast with grilled Portobello mushrooms too.

smoked haddock and spring onion coddled eggs

This is a very simple, quick dish. You can make it with many variations, replacing the haddock with crispy bacon bits, cooked mushrooms, prawns or spinach – even caviar. It's also great topped with a little smoked mozzarella or Gruyère cheese… Yummm!

SERVES 4

300g/10oz natural (undyed) smoked haddock
600ml/1 pint semi-skimmed milk
4 spring onions
butter, for greasing
8 eggs
salt and freshly ground black pepper

Preheat the oven to 180°C/350°F/gas 4. Put the haddock in a deep frying pan and pour the milk over it. Bring the milk to the boil over a medium heat. Simmer, covered, for 3–4 minutes, or until the fish is just cooked. Drain off and discard the milk. Remove the skin from the haddock and flake the flesh into small pieces. Finely chop the spring onions.

Generously grease 4 x 175ml/6fl oz ramekins with butter. Divide the flaked haddock and chopped spring onions between the ramekins. Carefully break 2 eggs into each dish, then put the dishes on a baking sheet and bake for 15 minutes until the eggs are just set. Season with salt and pepper.

Serve with a teaspoon and watch the yolks break over the haddock. Beautiful!

baked honey-rosewater figs with pistachios

This is a very pretty, quick breakfast dish, but it somehow still feels special.

SERVES 4
75g/3oz whole pistachios
8 figs
1 tbsp runny honey
1 tbsp rosewater
Greek yoghurt, to serve

Preheat the oven to 200°C/400°F/gas 6. Put the pistachios on a baking sheet and bake for 10–15 minutes, or until lightly roasted. Roughly chop the pistachios.

Cut each fig into quarters, but don't cut all the way through: they should still be intact at the base.

Place the figs on a baking sheet and drizzle with the honey. Bake for 10 minutes until bursting and caramelised. Take the figs out of the oven, put 2 on each plate and sprinkle with the rosewater and pistachios. Serve with a big dollop of Greek yoghurt.

bloody mary roasted tomatoes on garlic bruschetta

Great for Sunday mornings – this is what I like to eat if I'm hung-over! I always want something like toast to fill me up, yet I crave the chilli, garlic and sharpness of the tomatoes as a wake-up call. The vodka just gives it that extra edge. You needn't follow the measurements in this recipe too carefully – they should really be to your taste, so adapt freely.

SERVES 4

FOR THE ROASTED TOMATOES

750g/1½lb whole cherry tomatoes
2 tbsp vodka
1 tbsp Worcestershire sauce
4 dashes of Tabasco sauce
1 garlic clove, crushed
1 tsp balsamic vinegar
pinch each of sugar, salt and freshly ground
    black pepper
good glug of olive oil
1 tbsp shredded coriander
1 tbsp shredded basil

FOR THE BRUSCHETTA

4 slices of sour-dough bread (the French
    Poilâne is good)
olive oil
salt and freshly ground black pepper
2 garlic cloves, crushed

Preheat the oven to 200°C/400°F/gas 6. Mix all the roasted tomato ingredients together, apart from the herbs. Place on a baking sheet or in a baking dish and roast for 15–20 minutes, or until the tomatoes are bursting.

While the tomatoes are roasting, preheat the grill to high, or a griddle pan over a high heat. Sprinkle the slices of bread with a little olive oil and season with salt and pepper. Place on the griddle, or under the grill, and leave until starting to blacken. Turn over and do the same to the other side. Remove the bread from the heat and rub with the crushed garlic.

Take the tomatoes out of the oven, scatter with the herbs and toss together. Serve the bruschetta topped with the tomato mixture.

grilled portobello mushrooms with cheese-topped fried eggs

This a great vegetarian cooked breakfast. I devised the recipe so that my stepfather, who doesn't eat meat, could enjoy breakfast with the rest of the family.

SERVES 4

4 medium Portobello mushrooms
salt and freshly ground black pepper
olive oil, for frying
4 eggs
225g/8oz mature Cheddar cheese, grated
sweet chilli sauce or ketchup, to serve
    (optional)

Preheat the grill to high. Lay the mushrooms on a baking sheet, season with salt and pepper and drizzle with a little olive oil. Grill for 8–10 minutes.

Fry the eggs in a little olive oil and place one on top of each mushroom. Top with the grated Cheddar cheese and grill until hot and bubbling. If you're feeling very naughty, serve with sweet chilli sauce or – dare I say it? – ketchup.

sophie's super luxury muesli

Although a lot of chefs have created recipes for this, whenever I make my own muesli I'm amazed by the response – everyone seems to love it. It's good to prepare a big batch when you have time at the weekend, so you have it handy for the rest of the week.

MAKES 1.4KG/3LB 2OZ

500g/1lb jumbo rolled oats, preferably
   organic
225g/8oz bran flakes, preferably organic,
   sugar-free ones from a health-food shop
50g/2oz whole pistachios
125g/4oz unblanched almonds, coarsely
   chopped
125g/4oz dried cranberries
125g/4oz dried apricots, chopped
50g/2oz sultanas
50g/2oz sunflower seeds

Mix all of the ingredients together. Transfer the muesli to a large airtight container. It will keep for 2–3 months.

Serve with soya, rice or semi-skimmed milk or bio-yoghurt. You can also serve it soaked in apple juice, which is how it was made in the Swiss clinic where Bircher muesli originated.

more ideas

- Try mixing in some dried tropical fruits instead of the cranberries and apricots, such as papaya, mango, pineapple and banana chips with flaked coconut.

- Prunes, hazelnuts and yoghurt make a great extra topping, or blueberries and blackberries.

balinese coconut and banana pancakes

I tasted these for the first time whilst staying with my family in a place called Hidden Paradise on the north coast of Bali. It really was a dream retreat, with no one else for miles. We would go snorkelling surrounded by shoals of barracuda (until we found out how dangerous they were supposed to be) and then come back and tuck into some of the freshest fish I've ever had at a beach café. These pancakes became a favourite for breakfast, but I've adapted them to use less sugar. Frying the pancakes in coconut oil is what made them so distinctive and delicious, but they're still great with corn oil.

SERVES 4

FOR THE PANCAKES

50g/2oz oat, buckwheat or spelt flour
50g/2oz plain flour
pinch of salt
2 eggs, beaten
150ml/¼ pint skimmed milk
4 tbsp coconut oil or corn oil

FOR THE FILLING

2 tbsp Splenda sweetener
juice of 2 limes
grated zest of 1 lime
150g/5oz desiccated coconut
25g/1oz dark muscovado sugar
4 medium bananas

First, prepare the Splenda syrup for the filling. Heat 2 tablespoons water in a saucepan with the Splenda, lime zest and the juice of 1 lime until the Splenda has dissolved. Now make the pancakes. Sift both the flours and the salt into a bowl. Make a well in the middle of the flour, then whisk in the beaten eggs, milk and 75ml/3fl oz water. Let the batter rest for 10 minutes.

While the batter is resting, you can make the filling. Mix the coconut, Splenda syrup and muscovado sugar together into a soft moistened mixture. Preheat the oven to 200°C/400°F/gas 6.

Then make your pancakes. Put 1 tablespoon of the oil into a large frying pan over a high heat. When the oil is very hot, pour off any excess and turn the heat to medium. Pour a ladleful of the pancake batter into the pan and swirl it around to coat the base. Cook for about 3–4 minutes until golden brown, then flip the pancake over and cook the other side. Tip the pancake on to a plate and keep covered while you make 3 more.

Divide the coconut mixture between each pancake and spread evenly over the surface. Place a peeled banana in the centre of each pancake, squeeze some lime juice over the banana and roll up. Lay the pancakes on a baking sheet or in a baking dish, cover with foil and bake for 20 minutes, until heated through and the bananas have softened slightly.

the ultimate fruit platter

You may think this is too basic for words, but a well-done fruit platter makes a very luxurious breakfast. I've given extra fruit suggestions as the combination of fruit really does matter. This is where my perfectionist Virgo nature comes out!

SERVES 6
1 pineapple
1 mango
1 papaya
4 small bananas
4 passion fruit
2 persimmon
8 lychees
1 dragon fruit (mostly for the glorious pink colour…how glam is that!)
lime wedges, to serve

Find your most beautiful platter or dish. Prepare and cut up the fruit carefully and arrange it so that each type is grouped together, not mixed. Serve with lime wedges for squeezing over the fruit – so refreshing.

more ideas
- Create a big summer fruit platter with wedges of peaches, nectarines, different coloured melons and whole strawberries.
- Serve an autumn platter with plums, apples, pears and wild blackberries.

sweet cinnamon omelette with strawberries

This is as close to French cinnamon toast as I could muster. It tastes great and has far fewer carbs. There is something about cinnamon buns and muffins that send me crazy when I'm watching what I eat, but this curbs my sweet cinnamon cravings perfectly.

SERVES 1
3 eggs
1 tbsp semi-skimmed milk
1 tbsp Splenda sweetener
½ tsp cinnamon
knob of butter
125g/4oz strawberries, hulled and sliced
25g/1oz toasted flaked almonds

Preheat the grill to medium. Whisk the eggs and milk together. Stir in the sweetener and the cinnamon. Heat the butter in a small omelette pan. Pour in the egg mix and allow it to settle. Leave for about 1 minute, then fork it up, letting any uncooked mixture pour to the sides to cook.

Cook for about 3–4 minutes to set the bottom, then grill for 1 minute to finish cooking the top. Tip the strawberries into the middle, fold the omelette over and serve sprinkled with the flaked almonds.

asparagus with soft-boiled eggs and smoked salmon

As children, we all love eggs and soldiers. This is my grown-up version.

SERVES 4

salt and freshly ground black pepper
16 asparagus spears, ends trimmed
4 eggs
400g/13oz smoked salmon, preferably wild

Put a pan of lightly salted water on to boil for the asparagus, then cook the asparagus in the boiling water for 4–5 minutes until just tender, but still with a bit of bite.

While the asparagus is cooking, boil the eggs. Place them in another saucepan, cover with cold water, bring to the boil and cook for 3 minutes exactly.

Drain and season the asparagus. Lift the eggs from the water with a slotted spoon and peel them.

Divide the salmon between 4 plates. Lay the asparagus on the salmon and place the eggs on top of that. When each egg is cut, the runny yolk will spread all over the dish.

luscious lunches

This chapter is full of high-protein lunches. Most of the dishes are quite light with a good degree of variation. Obviously, the seared rump steak with wasabi hollandaise is high in saturated fats, whereas the grilled sardines with Mediterranean vegetables are high in healthy fish oils. So be intelligent about your choices and give yourself variety. It's all about balance. A little bit of what you fancy is okay, just no extremes.

One of the hardest parts of following a low-carb diet is snacks. Many of the light dishes in this chapter make ideal 'fillers', designed to sustain you any time you feel hungry. Don't forget: you can also choose a dinner recipe and have it for lunch, or vice versa, as both categories are protein-based. Plus, all the side orders can be eaten with the lunch or dinner protein choices.

smoked chicken, mango and avocado salad

You can keep a bowl of this in the fridge, ready to pick at when you're hungry.

SERVES 2 AS A LIGHT LUNCH AND
4-5 AS A SNACK
2 smoked chicken breasts
1 red or green chilli
1 mango
1 avocado
3 spring onions
1 tbsp chopped coriander
1 tsp chopped mint
juice of 2 limes
salt and freshly ground black pepper

Shred the chicken into smallish pieces. Deseed and finely chop the chilli. Peel, stone and dice the mango and avocado. Finely slice the spring onions. Mix together with the coriander and mint, then stir in enough lime juice to suit your taste. Season with salt and pepper.

pan-fried halloumi with salsa verde

A great light lunch, this dish can also make a good snack, providing a quick protein boost when you need it.

SERVES 2 AS A LIGHT LUNCH AND
4-5 AS A SNACK

250g8½oz block of halloumi cheese
lemon wedges, to serve

FOR THE SALSA VERDE

1 tbsp each roughly chopped parsley, mint and chives
1 tbsp capers
1 shallot
100ml/3½fl oz olive oil
finely grated zest and juice of 1 lemon
freshly ground black pepper

First make the salsa verde. Put the herbs in a small blender, then add the capers, shallot and olive oil and blitz together. Add the lemon zest and enough lemon juice and seasoning to taste.

Cut the halloumi into thick slices. Heat a heavy-based frying pan or griddle pan with no oil, then lightly fry each piece of cheese until golden brown on both sides.

Serve with lemon wedges for squeezing and the salsa verde. Any leftover salsa verde will keep for up to 2–3 days in the fridge and is great served with grilled meat.

roasted five-spice duck with spiced pears

Before I modified my eating habits, potato fondants were a real favourite. Unfortunately, they're full of fat and starch. Kohlrabi is a great replacement for potato and is an under-used vegetable.

SERVES 4

4 duck breasts, skin on
1 tsp five-spice powder
2 Asian pears, or regular pears
2 tbsp Splenda sweetener
2 star anise
½ tsp ground ginger
1 tsp Szechuan peppercorns (optional)
4 small kohlrabi
50g/2oz unsalted butter
900ml/1½ pints vegetable or chicken stock
4 small heads of bok choi
1–2 tbsp soy sauce

Score the skin of the duck breasts, rub with the five-spice powder and set aside.

Neatly peel, quarter and core the pears. Put the sweetener, star anise, ginger, peppercorns, if using, and 300ml/½ pint water in a medium saucepan and bring to the boil. Add the pears and simmer for about 15 minutes, or until just tender. Take off the heat and leave the pears in the syrup to cool.

Trim and peel the kohlrabi, cut into thick slices, then, using a plain round cutter, cut out rounds from the slices, of about 7.5cm/3in diameter.

Heat the butter in a non-stick frying pan, add the kohlrabi slices and brown them on each side. Pour in the stock and cover the pan with a piece of buttered greaseproof paper. Continue cooking until most of the stock has evaporated, about 30–40 minutes. Preheat the oven to 190°C/375°F/gas 5.

Meanwhile, put another frying pan on a very low heat and place the seasoned duck skin-side down in the pan. Cook on a low heat for about 15 minutes, pouring off the fat occasionally until no more runs out. Turn up the heat and brown off the duck skin, then turn the breasts over and seal the flesh side for about 4 minutes.

Start heating a steamer with water for the bok choi. Place the duck breasts on a baking sheet and roast, skin side up, for 6–8 minutes, until cooked through. Take them out of the oven, and let them rest, covered, for 10 minutes.

While the duck is resting, reheat the pears in their syrup and steam the bok choi in the steamer for 5 minutes. Drizzle the bok choi with the soy sauce.

To serve, divide the kohlrabi and bok choi between 4 plates. Slice the duck and arrange on top of the bok choi. Sit 2 pear quarters on each plate and serve.

lamb and feta burgers with tomato salad

This quick dish has a holiday feel. Since I was tiny, I've spent a lot of time in Greece. We now have a village house in Crete where the local food is superb, so I find Greek flavours come through a lot in my dishes. These burgers are also great for the barbecue.

SERVES 6

50g/2oz black olives, stoned
50g/2oz sun-dried tomatoes
2 garlic cloves
500g/1lb minced lamb
1 egg, beaten
1 tsp dried oregano
½ tsp dried rosemary
½ tsp dried crushed chilli flakes
salt and freshly ground black pepper
150g/5oz feta cheese
5 large ripe tomatoes
1 small red onion
small bunch of flat-leaf parsley
handful of mint leaves, roughly chopped
4 tbsp olive oil
juice of ½ lemon

Finely chop the olives, sundried tomatoes and garlic and mix in a bowl with the minced lamb. Mix in the egg, oregano, rosemary, chilli and some salt and pepper, then crumble in the feta. Carefully mix together, keeping the feta in pieces. Divide the mixture into 6, then shape into burgers and set aside.

Next prepare the salad. Roughly chop the tomatoes, thinly slice the onion and put them both in a bowl. Pick the leaves off the parsley and mix them together with the mint, the tomatoes and onion. Toss with 2 tablespoons of the olive oil and the lemon juice and season to taste.

Heat the remaining oil in a frying pan over a medium heat and fry the burgers for about 6 minutes on each side, until well-cooked through. Alternatively you can cook them on a barbecue. Serve with the tomato salad.

char-grilled marinated chicken

These delicious pieces of chicken are great to have on hand for lunch or for a snack between meals. You can buy something similar, ready-cooked, at most supermarkets, but it is often full of nasty additives. Far better to make your own. Three different marinades are suggested below, so you can ring the changes.

SERVES 4
4 skinless, boneless chicken breasts
green salad, to serve (optional)

honey and mustard marinade

1 tbsp olive oil
1 tbsp Dijon mustard
1 tbsp wholegrain mustard
1 tbsp runny honey

thai-inspired marinade

1 red chilli, finely sliced
1 garlic clove, crushed
5cm/2in piece of fresh root ginger, grated
finely grated zest and juice of 2 limes
½ tsp Thai fish sauce
3 tbsp coconut milk
1 tsp chopped coriander
1 tsp vegetable oil
pinch of salt

soy and sweet chilli marinade

3 tbsp soy sauce
1½ tsp sesame oil
2 tbsp sweet chilli sauce
1 spring onion, finely sliced
1 tsp sesame seeds

Cut the chicken into thickish strips and put in a glass bowl or dish. Make the marinade of your choice by mixing together the ingredients and add it to the chicken, working it through with your hands to coat evenly. Leave the chicken in the fridge for at least 1 hour, or overnight.

Heat a griddle pan or heavy-based frying pan and cook the chicken, turning occasionally, for about 5–8 minutes or until cooked through. Allow to cool and serve with a green salad, or store in the fridge to snack on. The chicken strips will keep for up to 2 days.

grilled lamb with spring vegetables and artichoke salad

This is a very colourful springtime dish. It looks lovely on a big platter – just invite everyone to dig in and serve themselves.

SERVES 4

6 baby carrots

6 baby turnips

6 patty pan squash

6 baby courgettes

6 baby pickling onions

4 lamb leg steaks

2 garlic cloves, crushed

5 tbsp olive oil

salt and freshly ground black pepper

12 asparagus spears, ends trimmed

8 cherry tomatoes, halved

400g/13oz can artichoke hearts, drained (or if fresh ones are available, see page 68 for preparation)

FOR THE PESTO

1 small garlic clove

75g/3oz basil leaves

50g/2oz roasted pine nuts

125g/4oz Parmesan cheese, finely grated

300ml/½ pint olive oil

First make the pesto. Put all the ingredients into a blender and blitz until well combined to a purée, or however you like the texture. Season with salt and pepper and set aside.

Now prepare the baby vegetables. This just means scrubbing and tidying up the carrots, turnips and patty pan squash, trimming the ends off the courgettes and peeling the onions.

Preheat a griddle pan or the grill. Rub the lamb steaks with the garlic, 1 tablespoon of the olive oil and some salt and pepper. Now grill or griddle for 6–8 minutes on each side. (I like my lamb very pink, but if you prefer yours a bit more cooked, griddle or grill it for a little longer.) Lift the meat on to a plate, cover with foil and leave it to rest. Put a large saucepan of salted water on to boil.

Add the carrots, turnips and baby onions to the boiling water and cook for 5 minutes. Then add the courgettes and patty pan squash and cook for a further 5 minutes. Finally, tip in the asparagus and cook for another 3–5 minutes or until the vegetables are just cooked. Drain them all and toss with the remaining olive oil, some seasoning, the cherry tomatoes and the artichoke hearts.

Cut the lamb into about 1cm/½in-thick slices. Arrange the vegetables on a platter or on individual plates with the meat and drizzle with the pesto. Any leftover pesto will keep chilled for up to a week.

shrimp saganaki

This is a very popular Greek dish. The best version I've ever tasted was at my favourite beach-side taverna Psaros, at Almirida, Crete. The secret ingredient that makes it work for me is the addition of the ouzo.

SERVES 4–6

1 onion
1 small fennel bulb, trimmed
2 garlic cloves
3 tbsp olive oil
2 x 400g/13oz cans chopped tomatoes
1 tbsp tomato purée
2 tsp dried oregano
100ml/3½fl oz ouzo (Greek aperitif)
500g/1lb cooked shelled king prawns
225g/8oz feta cheese
salt and freshly ground black pepper
green salad, to serve

Chop the onion and fennel into small pieces. Finely chop the garlic. Heat the oil in a large frying pan, then add the onion, fennel and garlic and fry until the onion is translucent. Stir in the tomatoes, tomato purée and oregano and cook for 20 minutes, uncovered, stirring occasionally until reduced to a thickish sauce.

Preheat the grill to high. Add the ouzo and prawns to the frying pan and bring to the boil. Simmer for 2 minutes to warm through and season to taste. Pour everything into a shallow heatproof dish and top with the crumbled feta. Grill until browned and serve with a green salad.

another idea

- For a change, you can also make this dish using cooked chicken instead of prawns.

coconut chicken salad

The freshness of Thai flavours makes tasty, healthy food. Garlic, chilli and ginger are natural decongestants (and aphrodisiacs!), so they're especially good if you are feeling in need of a little boost.

SERVES 4

4 skinless, boneless chicken breasts
5cm/2in piece of fresh root ginger
5cm/2in piece of galangal
2 garlic cloves
2 lemongrass stalks
1 small red chilli, deseeded
2 shallots
splash of corn or sunflower oil
200ml/7fl oz coconut cream
¼ tsp ground turmeric
2 bok choi
125g/4oz baby spinach leaves
1 mango
1 tsp Thai fish sauce
½ tsp palm sugar, Splenda sweetener or light muscovado sugar
salt and freshly ground black pepper
juice of 2 limes

FOR THE GARNISH
lime wedges
fresh coconut shavings (optional)
handful of chopped coriander

Dice the chicken into 2cm/¾in pieces. Coarsely grate the ginger, galangal and garlic. Finely chop the lemongrass and chilli. Thinly slice the shallots.

Heat a splash of oil in a deep frying pan or wok and fry the shallots until translucent. Add the lemongrass, garlic, galangal, ginger and chilli. Stir in the coconut cream and turmeric, bring to the boil and simmer for 4 minutes.

Tip in the chicken and cook for about 10 minutes, or until cooked through. While the chicken is cooking, prepare the salad leaves. Finely slice the bok choi but leave the baby spinach leaves whole. Put in a plastic bag and chill in the fridge. Peel and stone the mango and cut into small cubes.

Remove the chicken from the coconut cream with a slotted spoon. Stir the fish sauce and palm sugar, sweetener or muscovado sugar into the coconut cream. Heat until bubbling and allow it to thicken and reduce slightly so it will coat the chicken later. Taste to check if you need to add any further seasoning. Tip the chicken back into the sauce and stir in the mango cubes. Cool, then chill in the fridge.

Dress the salad leaves with enough lime juice to suit your taste and pile them on to 4 plates. Top with the chicken mix. Garnish with the lime wedges, coconut shavings, if using, and the coriander.

seared rump steak with wasabi hollandaise and chinese leaf salad

This is a quick, easy dish. Don't be put off by having to make the hollandaise sauce – as long as you follow the recipe, it won't fail. The wasabi just adds a nice bite and a more stylish touch. If you want to be really healthy, just miss out the hollandaise.

SERVES 4

½ head Chinese leaves (Chinese cabbage)
1 carrot
1 spring onion
1 red chilli, deseeded and finely diced
grated fresh root ginger
handful of coriander leaves, chopped
1 tbsp white rice vinegar
1 tbsp soy sauce
2–3 tbsp vegetable oil
splash of sesame oil
4 beef rump steaks
salt and freshly ground black pepper

FOR THE WASABI HOLLANDAISE

3 egg yolks
1 tsp white wine vinegar
150g/5oz unsalted butter, melted
splash of lemon juice
1 tsp wasabi (Japanese horseradish),
    or to taste

First make the salad. Finely slice the Chinese leaves and cut the carrot and spring onion into julienne strips. Mix all of these with the chilli, ginger, coriander, rice vinegar, soy sauce and both the oils. Set aside.

Make the hollandaise. In a metal bowl set over a pan of boiling water, whisk the egg yolks and wine vinegar until light and frothy. Gradually add the melted butter while whisking all the time, until you have a thick sauce. Now add a splash of hot water to thin the sauce down a little, and some lemon juice and wasabi to taste. Cover and keep warm.

Season the steaks well with salt and pepper. Heat a griddle pan or heavy-based frying pan until it is very hot, then sear the steaks for about 2 minutes on each side. Remove the steaks from the heat and leave to rest.

To serve, divide the salad between 4 plates. Slice the steaks, lay them on top of the salad and serve with a nice dollop of the hollandaise.

roast cod with baby à la grecque vegetables and saffron aïoli

Aïoli is basically a garlic mayonnaise made with olive oil. The saffron adds amazing colour and aroma. Aïoli is very strong and goes beautifully with lots of different dishes, such as crudités, king prawns and lamb kebabs.

SERVES 4

8 each of the following baby vegetables:
   turnip, carrot, leek, onion and patty pan
   squash
à la grecque ingredients (see page 147),
   omitting the artichokes
1 lemon
1-2 tbsp olive oil
4 cod steaks

FOR THE SAFFRON AIOLI

3 egg yolks
2 garlic cloves, crushed
1 tsp white wine vinegar
300ml/½ pint olive oil
juice of 1 lemon
salt and freshly ground black pepper
pinch of saffron threads

First prepare the baby vegetables – scrub and tidy up the turnips, carrots and patty pan squash, trim the ends off the leeks and peel the onions. Now put the à la grecque ingredients into a saucepan and pour in about 750ml/1¼ pints of water. Bring to the boil, then lower the heat and simmer for 10 minutes. Add the turnips and carrots and cook for 5 minutes, then add the remaining ingredients and cook for a further 15 minutes. Drain and set aside. (There is no need to chill the cooked vegetables in this recipe as they are served warm.)

Preheat the oven to 200°C/400°F/gas 6. Make the saffron aïoli. Place the egg yolks, crushed garlic and white wine vinegar into an electric blender and blitz together. Slowly pour in the olive oil until the mixture is thick and glossy. Then add the lemon juice and season with salt and pepper. Mix the saffron with 2 teaspoons boiling water and stir into the aïoli. Set aside.

Heat the 1–2 tablespoons olive oil in a large frying pan on a fairly high heat. Add the cod and fry briefly on both sides to brown quickly. Finish off by putting the fish on a baking sheet and roasting it in the oven for 10 minutes, or until cooked. Serve each cod steak with a spoonful of the aïoli and a little pile of the vegetables.

spring minestrone soup

Soups are very nourishing, they warm the soul, and this one is full of flavour. Change the vegetables according to whatever you have handy, or whatever is seasonal in your part of the world.

SERVES 4–6

3 rashers of bacon or pancetta
2 tbsp olive oil
1 onion, chopped
1 celery stick, chopped
1 leek, finely sliced
3 garlic cloves, crushed
100ml/3½fl oz white wine
2 litres/3½ pints stock
1 bay leaf
½ tsp dried oregano
1 courgette, sliced
50g/2oz French beans, cut into 5cm/2in pieces
1 head broccoli, broken into small florets
5 asparagus spears, chopped into 5cm/2in pieces
50g/2oz shelled broad beans
salt and freshly ground black pepper
½ tsp dried basil

TO SERVE

drizzle of chilli oil (see page 183) or extra-virgin olive oil
grated Parmesan cheese

Finely chop the bacon or pancetta. Heat the olive oil in a large saucepan, add the bacon, onion, celery, leek and garlic and fry until softened (about 5 minutes), but do not allow to colour. Add the wine, stock, bay leaf and oregano. Bring to the boil and simmer for 5 minutes.

Add the courgette and French beans and simmer for a further 5 minutes. Next add the broccoli, asparagus and broad beans and simmer for another 5 minutes. Check the seasoning and stir in the basil.

To serve, ladle the soup into bowls and sprinkle with chilli oil or extra-virgin olive oil, and Parmesan cheese.

french onion soup

When made well, this classic French dish tastes fantastic. My Mum used to make it for me and my brother, and it's been a firm favourite ever since.

SERVES 4

6 small to medium onions
125g/4oz butter
2 garlic cloves, crushed
200ml/7fl oz white wine
3 tbsp brandy
1 thyme sprig
1 bay leaf
1 litre/1¾ pints good-quality chicken stock
    (see page 180)
salt and freshly ground black pepper
Parmesan cheese shavings, to serve (optional)

Cut the onions in half and peel them. Then cut the base off each one and slice them very thinly from top to bottom. Melt the butter in a large saucepan and fry the onions and garlic for about 1 minute. Turn down the heat to low and cook until the onions are really soft and caramelised, stirring occasionally so they don't burn. This will take about 30 minutes. Don't rush this part of the recipe because this is what brings out the flavour.

Add the wine, brandy and herbs. Let the mixture bubble to cook off the alcohol, then pour in the stock. Bring to the boil, lower the heat and simmer, covered, for about 30 minutes, for all the flavours to amalgamate.

Taste for seasoning – if the stock is well flavoured, you may not need to add any. Serve topped with some Parmesan shavings if you like.

jerusalem artichoke and leek soup

This is a sustaining wintery comfort soup. Jerusalem artichokes have a lovely nutty flavour and smooth texture.

SERVES 4

1kg/2lb Jerusalem artichokes
squeeze of lemon juice
1 white onion
1 garlic clove
50g/2oz butter
1.5 litres/2½ pints chicken stock (see page 180)
salt and freshly ground black pepper
1 leek
50ml/2fl oz double cream

Peel and slice the artichokes into ½ cm/¼in slices, then leave them in a bowl of water with a squeeze of lemon juice to stop them discolouring. Finely chop the onion and garlic.

Melt the butter in a large saucepan and allow it to bubble until translucent, but not coloured. Turn down the heat to low, add the artichokes and leave them to sweat, covered, for 10 minutes, stirring occasionally.

Add the stock, bring to the boil and simmer for 20 minutes. Taste for seasoning – if the stock is well flavoured, you may not need to add any. Blitz in a liquidiser, or with a hand-blender and then pass through a sieve. Pour back into the pan.

Very finely slice the leek and add to the soup. Bring to the boil and simmer for 5 minutes. Add the cream, check the seasoning again and serve.

crab and tarragon salad

A lovely, special, light lunch dish. For the best taste, buy fresh crab meat from your fishmonger.

4 spring onions
600g/1lb 5oz fresh white crab meat
1 tbsp chopped tarragon leaves
2 tsp snipped chives
1 tsp finely chopped flat-leaf parsley
1–2 lemons, plus extra wedges to serve
splash of olive oil
dash of Tabasco
salt and freshly ground black pepper
2 heads of Little Gem lettuce

Slice the spring onions finely and mix with the crab and herbs. Finely grate the zest of 1 of the lemons and stir into the crab mix with lemon juice to taste. Mix in the olive oil, Tabasco and salt and pepper.

To serve, break up the lettuce into whole leaves (squeeze over a little lemon juice and add a splash of olive oil if you like). Divide the leaves between your plates and top with the crab mix. Serve with lemon wedges.

sesame-marinated tuna on a pickled ginger and mooli salad

Tuna is a very good source of omega-3 fish oils. Here the tuna is lightly seared rather than cooked through, and with the Japanese combination of flavours the whole dish tastes very fresh.

SERVES 4

1 tbsp wasabi (Japanese horseradish)
2 tbsp soy sauce
sesame oil
1 garlic clove, crushed
400g/13oz tail-end tuna loin
salt and freshly ground black pepper
50g/2oz sesame seeds
50g/2oz black onion seeds
½ mooli (Chinese white radish)
½ cucumber
125g/4oz pickled ginger (from a jar)
1 tsp white rice vinegar

Mix the wasabi, soy sauce, 1 teaspoon sesame oil and the crushed garlic together. Roll the tuna in this mixture, cover and marinate for about 2 hours.

When ready to cook, take the tuna out of the marinade, pat dry and season with pepper. Heat a frying pan until it is very hot, then sear the tuna just enough to see 5mm/¼in of 'cooked' tuna on the outside. Cool slightly.

Mix the sesame and onion seeds together. Roll the tuna loin in the seeds until evenly covered. Then roll the loin up tightly in clingfilm (to hold it together for slicing).

Peel the mooli and cut into thin julienne strips. Cut the cucumber in half lengthways and scoop out the seeds with a teaspoon. Finely slice the cucumber and pickled ginger and mix with the mooli. Season with salt, a splash of sesame oil and the rice vinegar.

To serve, pile the mooli salad on 4 plates. Thinly slice the tuna, then remove the clingfilm and lay the tuna slices on top of the salad.

scallops, artichokes and asparagus with caviar beurre blanc

This is a classy, very pretty lunch, but it also makes a sophisticated starter.

SERVES 4

16 large asparagus spears

4 globe artichokes, prepared and cooked (see page 147 for preparation, but cook for 30 minutes in boiling water instead, with the juice of 1 lemon added)

12 scallops (ask your fishmonger for ones that haven't been frozen)

1 tbsp olive oil

1 lemon, for squeezing

FOR THE CAVIAR BEURRE BLANC

100ml/3½fl oz white wine vinegar

1 tbsp double cream

150g/5oz cold unsalted butter

juice of 1 lemon

1 tbsp caviar (sevruga is cheaper and fine for this dish)

salt and freshly ground black pepper

Prepare the vegetables. Peel the asparagus spears, (being careful not to peel too deeply), leaving 2.5cm/1in of stalk unpeeled at the ends. Trim off these ends and halve each asparagus spear widthways. Cut the prepared and cooked artichoke bases into quarters and set aside. Put a large pan of water on to boil for the asparagus.

To prepare the scallops, leave the corals (orange sacs) on or take them off if you prefer. (I usually take the corals off and pan-fry them separately in some *beurre noisette* – nut-brown butter – with a few capers.) Season the scallops and set them aside on a plate until ready to cook.

Next make the *beurre blanc* sauce. Put the vinegar in a medium saucepan and boil to reduce by two thirds: this takes about 8–10 minutes. Slowly pour in the cream – this acts as a stabiliser. Cut the butter into small cubes and whisk in 2 pieces at a time until it is fully amalgamated. In between each butter addition, put the pan back on the heat to warm through, but do not allow it to boil. When all the butter has been added, you should have a thick, glossy sauce. Squeeze in the lemon juice, stir in the caviar, then season. This sauce must not get too cold or too hot, so keep it covered in a warm place, but not on a direct heat or it may separate.

Check that the large saucepan of water is boiling rapidly, then add the asparagus. Cook for about 4–5 minutes, or until the base of the asparagus is tender, but still crunchy. Do not overcook.

While the asparagus is cooking, pour the olive oil into a frying pan and heat until very hot. Add the scallops to the pan and cook for about 2 minutes on each side until they turn golden and caramelise: this brings out the sweet flavour. Season again and squeeze over a little lemon juice.

Arrange the scallops, asparagus and artichokes on plates and drizzle with the beurre blanc. Enjoy!

lobster and mango salad with coriander-chilli dressing

This is a very impressive, luxury weekend lunch dish. I love the colours and almost stark beauty of the lobster, spinach and mango. I've used cooked lobster in this recipe, as it is often difficult to find live lobster, but if you want to prepare and cook your own, see page 186.

SERVES 4

small handful of coriander
2 egg yolks
1 tbsp white wine vinegar
50ml/2fl oz light olive oil
100ml/3½fl oz vegetable oil
juice of 1 lime
1 red chilli, deseeded and finely chopped
1 mango
2 lobsters, about 1kg/2lb each, cooked
about 225g/8oz baby spinach leaves
2–3 tbsp olive oil
squeeze of lemon juice
salt and freshly ground black pepper
lime wedges, to garnish

Finely chop most of the coriander, leaving a few whole leaves for the garnish. You need to make a light mayonnaise first. Do this by putting the egg yolks and wine vinegar into a food processor. Switch it on and gradually pour in the oils through the top. Do not add the oils too quickly, or the mayonnaise will separate. Add the chopped coriander towards the end. Squeeze in the lime juice and mix in the chopped chilli. Finally, mix in about 2 tablespoons warm water until the consistency is smooth and as thick as you like it. It should be slightly runny, a bit like a thick Caesar salad dressing. Pour the dressing into a container and chill. (It will keep for up to 3 days and you will probably have some left over.)

Peel, stone and dice the mango and set aside. Using a large chopping board and a large, sharp chef's knife, cut the lobster between the eyes. Then cut right down the middle, dividing it completely in half. Very gently remove all the meat, keeping it in one piece. To remove the claw meat, crack the shell with the base of a knife and gently extract the meat. You should allow half a tail and 1 claw per person. There is also meat in the legs, but it is the chef's privilege to eat this to keep you going while you are cooking.

Dress the spinach leaves in the olive oil, lemon juice and seasoning. Place the spinach leaves on 4 plates. Arrange the lobster meat on top and scatter the mango cubes over. Drizzle with lots of dressing and garnish with the reserved coriander leaves and the lime wedges.

chicken liver, walnut and pomegranate salad

Chicken livers are very high in iron and are delicious in a salad. Walnuts contain calcium and magnesium, and they reduce potentially harmful serum cholesterol levels. They are also recognised as an aphrodisiac in Greek cuisine. All good enough reasons to eat them, I reckon! Pomegranate molasses is available in Middle Eastern stores and good delis. Of course you can leave it out if you can't find any.

SERVES 4

5 tbsp extra-virgin olive oil

1 tbsp red wine vinegar

1 tbsp pomegranate molasses

salt and freshly ground black pepper

50g/2oz walnuts

1 pomegranate

500g/1lb chicken livers, trimmed and cleaned

about 175g/6oz mixed salad leaves, such as
    baby chard, mizuna and rocket

Make the dressing by whisking together 2 tablespoons of the olive oil, the red wine vinegar, pomegranate molasses and some seasoning. Set aside.

Break up the walnuts into slightly smaller pieces and roast in a dry frying pan until golden all over, tossing often. Cut the pomegranate in half and tap out the seeds. Pick through the seeds and remove any bits of pith. Set aside.

Heat the frying pan again and add the remaining olive oil. Season the livers and fry them on a high heat for about 5 minutes, until they are golden-brown on the outside, yet still quite pink on the inside.

In a large bowl, mix the leaves with the dressing, then divide between 4 plates. Top with the chicken livers and sprinkle with the walnuts and pomegranate seeds.

sea bass and scallops with fennel, carrot and sauternes fricassée

This is a lovely dish. Scallops, when cooked well, are a true pleasure. They should have a beautiful golden brown crust on the outside and be just cooked in the middle.

SERVES 4

2 small fennel bulbs
4 banana or regular shallots
4 carrots
50g/2oz butter
5 tbsp olive oil
2 large pinches of saffron threads
200ml/7fl oz Sauternes wine
juice of 2 oranges
100ml/3½fl oz fish stock (shop-bought is fine)
150ml/¼ pint carton double cream
salt and freshly ground black pepper
1 tbsp chopped tarragon leaves
4 sea bass fillets, preferably wild
6 large scallops, sliced in half

Carefully and finely slice the fennel, shallots and carrots (across, not lengthways) – a mandolin is best for this. Heat the butter and 2 tablespoons of the olive oil in a large saucepan, tip in the sliced vegetables and, when they start to go translucent, stir in the saffron and wine. Allow the mixture to bubble away until the wine is reduced by half.

Pour in the orange juice, fish stock and cream and continue simmering until the carrots, fennel and shallots are cooked, but still have a slight bite. Scoop them out with a slotted spoon and set aside, leaving the liquid in the pan. Continue to reduce this until half the original amount remains. Season to taste with salt and pepper.

Mix the vegetables and chopped tarragon with enough of the sauce so they are just coated. Keep warm. Reserve the rest of the sauce in a bowl and keep warm.

Heat a frying pan until very hot, add 2 more tablespoons of the olive oil and then the sea bass, skin-side down. Fry for 4 minutes until the skin is crisp, then turn over and cook for 4 minutes on the other side. Season. Remove the fish and keep it warm. Pour the rest of the oil into the pan and turn up the heat. Sear the scallops on both sides, cooking for 5 minutes, turning half-way through, until they are golden-brown and caramelised.

To serve, spoon a pile of the sauced vegetables in the middle of each plate. Top each with a sea bass fillet and 3 scallop pieces. Froth up the reserved sauce with a hand blender, spoon around the vegetables and serve.

gado-gado with shredded chicken

This is a traditional Indonesian dish to which I
have added chicken. It usually consists of a platter
of different vegetables and hard-boiled eggs,
topped with peanut sauce. Use whatever
combination of vegetables you have to hand –
this is just a guide.

SERVES 4
FOR THE GADO-GADO SAUCE
1 small shallot
1 garlic clove
1 tbsp vegetable oil
¼ tsp chilli powder
150g/5oz crunchy peanut butter
juice of 1 lime
3 tbsp soy sauce

FOR THE SALAD
4 eggs
3 skinless, boneless chicken breasts
750ml/1¼ pints chicken stock (see page 180)
¼ white cabbage
125g/4oz bean sprouts
1 cucumber
225g/8oz French beans
salt and freshly ground black pepper

TO GARNISH
1 red chilli, deseeded and finely sliced
good handful of torn coriander leaves
lime wedges

Make the gado-gado sauce. Finely chop the
shallot and garlic. Heat the vegetable oil and
lightly fry the shallot and garlic until translucent.
Add the chilli powder, then take off the heat and
stir in the peanut butter, lime juice, soy sauce and
200ml/7fl oz warm water. Return to the heat and
warm through gently. You should have a thickish
sauce. Remove and set aside.

Next prepare the salad ingredients. Hard-boil the
eggs (see page 187) and peel them. Then put the
chicken in a deep frying pan and add the stock.
Bring to the boil and simmer for 10 minutes.
Take off the heat and leave the chicken to cool
completely in the stock.

Meanwhile, put a saucepan of water on to boil
for the beans. Finely slice the cabbage and mix
with the bean sprouts in a large bowl. Cut the
cucumber in half lengthways and scoop out the
seeds. Cut the cucumber into thin diagonal slices,
then mix with the cabbage and bean sprouts.
Cook the French beans in the boiling water for
3–4 minutes until tender-crisp, then drain and
refresh under running cold water. Tip them into
the other salad vegetables. Season to taste.

Take the chicken out of the poaching liquid and
shred it into pieces. Quarter the hard-boiled eggs.

To serve, put a big pile of salad in the centre of
each plate. Top with the chicken and then spoon
over the gado-gado sauce. Sprinkle with the chilli
and coriander leaves. Garnish with the egg
quarters and lime wedges and serve.

celeriac rémoulade with shredded ham

You can save the ham cooking liquid from this recipe and use it for other dishes. In Ireland they cook cabbage in it, or you can use it as a stock base for ham and pea soup.

SERVES 4

1 ham hock, about 700g/1½ lb in weight
1 celery stick
1 onion
1 carrot
1 leek
2 bay leaves
whole black peppercorns

FOR THE RÉMOULADE
1 celeriac
2 apples
2 tbsp mayonnaise
1½ tbsp wholegrain mustard
1 tsp Dijon mustard
salt and freshly ground black pepper

Soak the ham in cold water for a couple of hours to remove some of the salt, then drain off the water. (Alternatively, you can put it in a saucepan of cold water, bring it to the boil and then drain it off.)

Roughly chop all the vegetables and place in the saucepan with the ham. Add the bay leaves and peppercorns, cover with fresh water and bring to the boil. Cover and cook for about 40 minutes (allow about 25 minutes per 500g/1lb), plus an extra 25 minutes at the end. When cooked, drain off the water and leave the ham to cool.

Meanwhile prepare the rémoulade. Put another, smaller saucepan of water on to boil. Peel the celeriac, then cut it into very thin julienne strips and blanch in boiling water for 2 minutes. Drain and refresh under running cold water. Peel and core the apple and cut into julienne strips as well.

Mix the celeriac, apple, mayonnaise and mustards together. Season lightly – don't over-season, as the ham will still be quite salty. Take the fat off the cooled ham hock and shred the meat. Serve with the rémoulade.

tandoori-style monkfish with cucumber raita

Monkfish is a lovely, meaty fish which takes on strong flavours well. It's fantastic in curries and even roasted whole, like a joint of meat. Here I've coated it in spices and roasted it. It's actually a Moroccan-cross-Indian dish – the preserved lemons really complement the rich flavour of the fish.

SERVES 4

800g/1¾lb monkfish tail
2 tbsp tandoori paste
½ cucumber
small handful of mint leaves
300ml/½ pint natural live yoghurt
3 preserved lemons
1 red chilli
1 tbsp chopped fresh coriander
1 tbsp toasted cumin seeds
1 tbsp vegetable oil

Cut the monkfish into 4 large pieces. Rub all over with the tandoori paste and put in an ovenproof dish or on a small baking sheet. Leave in the fridge to marinate for at least 30 minutes.

Preheat the oven to 200°C/400°F/gas 6. Peel, then coarsely grate the cucumber, finely chop the mint and mix together with the yoghurt to make the raita. Cut the lemons into small pieces. Deseed and finely chop the chilli. Mix the lemons and chilli together with the coriander and the cumin seeds.

Drizzle the fish with the oil and roast for 15–20 minutes, or until cooked through. Serve with a dollop of raita and the preserved lemon mixture.

thai chicken curry

This is a modern-day classic. It seems possible to get this dish everywhere nowadays, from pubs to cafés, but there are curries and CURRIES... This one is very fresh-tasting and absolutely delicious.

SERVES 4

mix of 8–10 chicken thighs and legs
salt and freshly ground black pepper
3 tbsp vegetable oil
4 shallots, finely chopped
2 tbsp grated fresh root ginger
2 tbsp crushed garlic
1 tbsp grated galangal
2 tbsp finely chopped lemongrass
1 tsp finely chopped red chilli
1 tsp ground turmeric
750ml/1¼ pints chicken stock (see page 180)
400ml/14fl oz can coconut milk
5 kaffir lime leaves
lime juice, to taste
1 mango, peeled, stoned and cubed (optional)
handful of coriander, chopped

Season the chicken with salt and pepper. Heat 2 tablespoons of the oil in a large saucepan, add the chicken and cook until golden brown all over. Remove the chicken from the pan and set aside.

Heat the rest of the oil in the pan and fry the shallots, ginger, garlic, galangal, lemongrass, chilli and turmeric, until the shallots have softened. Pour in the stock and coconut milk, then return the chicken to the pan with the lime leaves. Simmer for about 30–40 minutes, or until the chicken is tender.

Add lime juice to taste and the mango, if using, and toss in the coriander leaves.

duck and lychee salad
with szechuan peppercorn dressing

Feeling inspired after a visit to Beijing, this is my attempt to introduce some lovely Chinese flavours into your cooking.

SERVES 4

4 duck breasts
5 spring onions
2 carrots
¼ cucumber
400g/13oz can lychees, drained
225g/8oz bean sprouts
225g/8oz baby spinach
salt and freshly ground black pepper

FOR THE DRESSING

1 tsp cracked Szechuan peppercorns
2 tbsp white rice vinegar
2 tsp plum sauce
2 tsp sweet soy sauce
2 tsp soy sauce

Preheat the oven to 190°C/375°C/gas 5. Score the duck skin, season with salt and pepper, and place the breasts in a frying pan on a low heat. Cook slowly, skin-side down, for about 15 minutes, pouring off the fat occasionally, until all the fat has cooked out.

Turn up the heat and brown off the duck skin, then turn over and brown on the flesh side for about 4 minutes. Put the duck breasts on a baking sheet and roast, skin side up, for 6–8 minutes, or until cooked through. Take them out of the oven and allow them to rest, covered, for 10 minutes.

While the duck is resting, make the dressing. Dry-fry the peppercorns in a small pan, then add the rice vinegar, plum sauce and the soy sauces and bring just to the boil. Take off the heat and leave to cool.

Cut the spring onions and the carrots into thin strips and mix together. Cut the cucumber in half lengthways, scoop out the seeds, then cut the cucumber into thin diagonal slices. Tear the lychees into rough pieces, discarding the stones. Mix all the vegetables and lychees with the bean sprouts and spinach. Pour some of the dressing on to the salad and toss together.

Slice the duck breasts and serve on top of the salad. Drizzle with a bit of extra dressing.

courgettes and aubergines stuffed with spiced cheeses

This very simple vegetarian dish is lovely served with a green salad and some thinly sliced tomatoes.

SERVES 4

2 tsp cumin seeds
300g/10oz feta cheese
300g/10oz soft goat's cheese
1 bunch of spring onions, finely sliced
1 tbsp mango chutney
salt and freshly ground black pepper
2 small aubergines
2 medium courgettes
a little olive oil

Preheat the oven to 180°C/350°/gas 4. Dry-fry the cumin seeds in a small frying pan until the spicy aroma comes out. Crumble the feta and the goat's cheese into a bowl and mix in the cumin seeds, spring onions and mango chutney. Season to taste – you probably won't need salt.

Cut the aubergines and courgettes in half lengthways, scoop out the seeds and flesh and discard. Rub the aubergines and courgettes with salt, pepper and olive oil. Place the vegetable shells on separate baking trays or in separate ovenproof dishes and spoon in the cheese mixture to fill them. Place the tray of aubergines in the oven first, then add the tray of courgettes after 10 minutes. Bake for another 20–30 minutes, or until the vegetables are tender.

griddled sardines on mediterranean vegetables

Sardines are very under-rated. When fresh, they are full of flavour and omega-3 fish oils which are very good for your health. Add the lightly cooked vegetables and lycopene-rich tomatoes and you have a vibrant, vitamin-packed meal.

SERVES 4

250g/8½oz cherry tomatoes
2 garlic cloves, crushed
75ml/3fl oz olive oil, plus 3–4 tbsp
2 tsp balsamic vinegar
salt and freshly ground black pepper
1 red pepper
1 yellow pepper
1 courgette
1 aubergine
1 red onion
8 fresh sardines
good handful of basil, shredded

Preheat the oven to 200°C/400°/gas 6. Toss the tomatoes with the garlic, the 75ml/3fl oz olive oil, the balsamic vinegar and seasoning in a baking dish or on a baking sheet and roast for 20 minutes or until starting to burst.

Meanwhile, core and deseed the peppers and chop into large pieces. Slice the courgettes and aubergines and quarter the onion. Put all the vegetables into a bowl, season and rub with about 2 tablespoons olive oil. Put a griddle pan or other heavy-based pan on to heat.

When the griddle is very hot, sear the vegetables on each side. This is really to get good 'charcoal marks', not to cook throughout. Then transfer the vegetables to a baking sheet and finish in the oven for 6 minutes until softened.

Brush the sardines with the remaining olive oil and season. Lay them on the hot griddle and cook for 5 minutes on each side. Take off the heat and set aside to rest for a few minutes, covered.

Remove the tomatoes from the oven and stir in the basil. Arrange the vegetables in the centre of each plate and top with the sardines. Spoon some of the tomatoes and their juices over the sardines and serve.

pan-roast wild salmon on pea and tarragon crush

This dish really is summer on a plate. I love the pretty colours of pastel pink and green together. The shrimp dressing is the final touch that sets off the whole dish.

SERVES 4
4 salmon fillets, preferably wild or organic, skin on

FOR THE PEA AND TARRAGON CRUSH
200ml/7fl oz vegetable stock
500g/1lb frozen peas
1½ tbsp chopped tarragon

FOR THE SHRIMP DRESSING
olive oil
1 shallot, finely chopped
1 garlic clove, crushed
pinch of ground mace
pinch of grated nutmeg
100ml/3½fl oz white wine
125g/4oz butter, cut into pieces
250g/8½oz cooked shelled brown shrimps
2 tsp chopped flat-leaf parsley
lemon juice, to taste
salt and freshly ground black pepper

Make the shrimp dressing. Heat 1 tablespoon olive oil in a small pan and fry the shallot and garlic with the mace and nutmeg until the shallot is translucent. Add the wine and butter and, when the butter has melted, boil rapidly for about 4 minutes to amalgamate. Remove from the heat, stir in the shrimps, parsley and lemon juice to taste. Season and set aside.

Make the pea and tarragon crush. Bring the stock to the boil in a medium saucepan. Tip in the peas and cook for about 3 minutes. Remove from the heat, drain off and discard two thirds of the liquid, then crush the peas with a potato masher. Add the chopped tarragon and season to taste.

Heat a non-stick frying pan to a medium heat. Brush the salmon with some olive oil and season. Place the salmon skin-side down in the pan and cook for about 7 minutes until you get a crisp, golden crust, then turn the salmon over and cook for a further 3 minutes. While the salmon is cooking, gently reheat the shrimp dressing and the pea crush.

To serve, place a pile of the pea crush in the middle of each plate, lay the salmon on top and spoon the shrimp dressing over the salmon and around the crush.

smoked trout, roasted baby beetroot and horseradish salad

This classic flavour combination of smoked fish, beetroot and horseradish really works. It always reminds me of New York delis like Zabars. I love New York – I feel as if I'm on a movie set the whole time, with all the steam rising from the grates in the roads and yellow taxis flying past. The food is amazing too, and I'm getting wander-lust just thinking about it!

SERVES 4

12 baby beetroot
2 tbsp olive oil
125g/4oz soured cream
2 tbsp hot horseradish sauce
½ small bunch of chives
1 small red onion
4 smoked trout fillets, skinned
selection of baby salad leaves, such as red chard, rocket or whatever you prefer

FOR THE DRESSING

1 tbsp olive oil
juice of ½ lemon
salt and freshly ground black pepper

Preheat the oven to 200°C/400°F/gas 6. Trim the beetroot, then drizzle with the olive oil, season with salt and pepper and place on a baking sheet. Roast for 30–40 minutes until tender.

Meanwhile, beat the soured cream and horseradish together and set aside. Snip the chives into 5cm/2in lengths. Finely slice the red onion. Break the trout into large pieces and set aside. Mix together all the dressing ingredients and set aside.

Toss the salad leaves, onion and chives together. When the beetroot is cooked, peel off the skin. Season the salad leaves and dress with as much dressing as needed.

Divide the salad leaves among 4 plates, top with the smoked trout and a dollop of the soured cream and horseradish mixture. Arrange the beetroot around the plates and serve.

another idea

- If you can't find raw beetroot, you can use pre-cooked. Avoid using beetroot in vinegar, though, as this will overpower the flavour of the dish.

cod on roasted fennel with squid, mussel and saffron sauce

This dish looks nothing short of fabulous – and it tastes pretty special too! The colour of the sauce makes a great contrast to the mussel shells.

SERVES 4

1 large fennel bulb, cut into eighths
3 tbsp olive oil
salt and freshly ground black pepper
8 baby squid tubes, cleaned
750ml/1¼ pints fish stock (see page 181)
2 large pinches of saffron threads
500g/1lb mussels in their shells, cleaned
2 garlic cloves, finely chopped
2 shallots, finely chopped
200ml/7fl oz white wine
3 plum tomatoes
1 tsp finely chopped tarragon
1 tsp finely chopped basil
4 cod fillets, skin on

Preheat the oven to 180°C/350°F/gas 4. Put the fennel on a baking sheet, sprinkle with 2 tablespoons of the olive oil, season and bake for 25–30 minutes, or until tender. Cover the fennel and keep it warm.

Very finely slice the squid into rings. Heat the fish stock and saffron in a saucepan. Add the squid rings. Bring to the boil, then turn down the heat and simmer for 20–30 minutes, or until tender. Drain the squid in a sieve or colander placed over

a bowl, keep the liquid and pour it back into the pan. Bring to the boil, then boil until reduced by two thirds. Reserve the squid.

In a separate saucepan (one big enough to hold the mussels), heat the remaining olive oil until very hot and quickly add the mussels, garlic, shallots and wine. Cover the pan and cook until all the mussels are open, about 3–5 minutes, discarding any that do not open. Take out the mussels and add the mussel cooking liquid to the reduced fish stock. Pick the meat out of two thirds of the mussels and add this and the squid to the stock mixture. Reserve the remaining unshelled mussels.

Quarter the tomatoes, scoop out the seeds and discard. Dice the flesh into neat squares. Add the diced tomatoes to the mussel and squid sauce along with the herbs. Check the seasoning.

In a frying pan, cook the cod skin-side down for 6 minutes, then finish on the flesh side for 3 minutes, although the timing depends on how thick the cod is.

Add the reserved unshelled mussels to the sauce and gently heat through. Divide the fennel between 4 plates, top with the cod and spoon the mussel and squid sauce around each plate, arranging the shells prettily.

dolcelatte-stuffed chicken with pumpkin mash

I love the way the saltiness of the dolcelatte in this dish complements the sweet pumpkin mash.

SERVES 4

4 skinless, boneless chicken breasts
4 slices of prosciutto or Parma ham
225g/8oz dolcelatte cheese
1 small pumpkin or squash
3–4 tbsp olive oil
salt and freshly ground black pepper
rocket salad, to serve

Preheat the oven to 200°C/400°F/gas 6. Slice each chicken breast through the middle so you can open it out into a 'butterfly' shape. Spread the prosciutto or Parma ham slices on a work surface and place a chicken breast on each. Divide the cheese into four and put 1 piece in the centre of each chicken breast. Fold up the chicken so it is wrapped in the ham and set aside.

Peel and deseed the pumpkin or squash. Cut the flesh into cubes and put on a baking sheet. Drizzle with 2 tablespoons of the olive oil and season with salt and pepper. Roast for 30–40 minutes, or until golden and tender.

Ten minutes before the squash is cooked, heat a frying pan until very hot, add the rest of the oil and fry the wrapped chicken breasts until golden on each side. Lay them on a baking sheet and roast in the oven for 15 minutes.

While the chicken finishes roasting, roughly mash the pumpkin or squash and season. Remove the chicken from the oven and cut each breast into about 5 slices. Place a dollop of mash on each plate, arrange the chicken over it and serve with some rocket leaves on the side.

anchovy, roasted pepper and black olive salad

This is very colourful and good to do as part of a buffet as it can be made the day before. It's also a great source of those valuable omega-3 fish oils.

SERVES 6
3 red peppers
3 yellow peppers
4 tbsp olive oil
salt and freshly ground black pepper
small handful of basil leaves, roughly torn
225g/8oz marinated anchovies
125g/4oz black olives, stoned

Preheat the oven to 220°C/425°F/gas 7. Place the whole peppers on a baking sheet and roast for 30 minutes, until charred and softened. Remove from the oven and tip the peppers into a large mixing bowl. Cover with clingfilm and leave to cool. (This makes them easier to peel.) Reserve any of the pepper roasting juices and mix with the olive oil, seasoning and basil. Set aside.

Peel and deseed the peppers, then cut them into wide strips. Lay the peppers on a platter, or on individual plates. Arrange the anchovies on top, scatter the olives over, then drizzle with the basil oil.

manchego, parma ham and membrillo skewers

Throughout this chapter you will find several recipes that make great snacks. This is one of them. The creamy manchego cheese goes perfectly with the membrillo (a fragrant quince jelly, from Spain) and the salty ham.

MAKES APPROX. 12 SKEWERS
225g/8oz manchego cheese
125g/4oz membrillo (quince jelly)
6 slices of prosciutto or Parma ham, about
    90g/3¼oz

Cut the manchego cheese into 12 cubes and the membrillo into 12 smaller-sized cubes. Cut each slice of prosciutto or Parma ham in half length-ways and wrap each piece around a cube of cheese.

Thread a cube of wrapped cheese and a cube of membrillo on to cocktail sticks and serve.

another idea

- If you can't find membrillo, these skewers are also delicious made with figs, semi-dried prunes or mustard fruits instead.

artichoke, goat's cheese and asparagus tartlets

This recipe came about because I wanted to make a miniature tartlet without pastry. Instead, I used naturally cup-like artichoke bases and filled them with goat's cheese, asparagus and a quiche-like egg mix – *et voilà*: a no-carbs tart!

SERVES 4
4 large globe artichokes
lemon juice
1 litre/1¾ pints tomato juice
¼ bottle white wine
2 tbsp olive oil, plus a little extra
salt and freshly ground black pepper
12 very thin asparagus tips (they must be the tiny ones so they fit in the artichoke cases)
2 smoked bacon rashers
1 small shallot, finely chopped
1 egg
2 tbsp semi-skimmed milk
125g/4oz goat's cheese, crumbled
dressed salad leaves, to serve

First, prepare the artichokes. Pare down each artichoke base. Using a sharp knife, slice the stem off at the base, then snap the leaves off one by one and discard them. Use a smaller knife to trim the base, taking off any dark green bits. Rub the artichokes with lemon juice to stop them discolouring.

Put the prepared artichokes in a saucepan with the tomato juice, white wine, olive oil, a splash of lemon juice and seasoning. Bring to the boil, then lower the heat and simmer for 20–30 minutes, or until the artichoke bases are tender enough for a knife to slide into them easily. Remove from the heat and leave to cool in the tomato mixture.

Cut the asparagus tips into 2.5cm/1in lengths. Put a small pan of water on to boil and blanch the tips for 1 minute, then refresh under cold water, drain and set aside. Cut the bacon into small pieces and fry until crispy, adding the chopped shallot half-way through.

Preheat the oven to 200°C/400°F/gas 6. Beat the egg and milk together and season. Take the artichoke bases out of the liquid and rinse under warm water. Pat them dry, then take off any remaining leaves, scoop out the furry choke and tidy up the edges with a sharp knife. Brush them lightly with oil and place on a baking sheet.

Start building up your tartlets. Crumble a little goat's cheese into each artichoke base, sprinkle on some of the bacon mix and stick in the asparagus tips. Then gently spoon in the egg mix to fill them up. Bake for 20 minutes until the filling is set, and serve on top of the dressed salad leaves.

another idea

- For a vegetarian option, omit the bacon and asparagus and add chopped pan-fried wild mushrooms and a little truffle oil instead.

sake–and–vanilla–cured salmon

This dish was inspired by a trip to Japan and Australia – the flavours are unusual, but they work really well together. The sake and salt/sugar mixture 'cures' the salmon and the vanilla gives it an interesting and rounded flavour.

SERVES 6–8

½ side of very fresh salmon, about
    500-750g/1lb-1½ lb
200ml/7fl oz Japanese sake
2 vanilla pods
finely grated zest of 1 lemon
2 tbsp salt
1 tbsp golden caster sugar
2 spring onions
150ml/¼ pint soured cream
freshly ground black pepper

TO SERVE
lemon wedges
cucumber relish (see page 86)

Put the salmon in a large, deep dish, with the side where the skin was uppermost. Pour in the sake and leave for 30 minutes. Take the salmon out of the sake and gently pat it dry. Discard the sake and return the salmon to the dish.

Split the vanilla pods lengthways and scrape out the seeds. Mix the vanilla seeds, lemon zest, salt and sugar together and spread evenly all over the salmon. Cover tightly with clingfilm, place a weight on top (a chopping board will do) and chill in the fridge for 2 days.

Finely slice the spring onions and mix with the soured cream and black pepper to taste. Set aside.

Take the salmon from the fridge and brush off all the salt, sugar and lemon mix. Then, with a very sharp knife, cut the salmon as thinly as possible on a slant, so you get nice, fine slices. Serve each portion with a lemon wedge, a dollop of the soured cream mix and some cucumber relish.

chilli and garlic king prawns

Chilli and garlic are nature's remedies. Both act as major decongestants and both contain anti-oxidants. This versatile dish could be used as a light lunch or a starter, or kept in the fridge as a snack to nibble on.

SERVES 2

250g/8½oz cooked shelled king prawns
1 small red chilli, deseeded and finely chopped
1 garlic clove, finely chopped
1 tsp chopped basil
1 tsp chopped parsley
juice of 1 lemon
3 tbsp olive oil

Mix everything together and marinate for as long as you can bear (up to an hour), then...tuck in!

monkfish and chorizo kebabs on pepperonata

This is sunshine on a plate. It makes me think of Spain. It's like a tapas combo.

SERVES 4

3 red peppers
3 yellow peppers
2 onions
3 garlic cloves
4 tbsp olive oil
4 plum tomatoes, quartered
1 pinch of saffron threads
1 tsp golden caster sugar or Splenda sweetener
1 tbsp chopped fresh basil
1 tbsp small capers
salt and freshly ground black pepper
4 small chorizo sausages, each 5cm/2in long
500g/1lb monkfish, cut into large cubes

An hour before you are ready to start cooking, soak 8 wooden skewers in cold water.

For the pepperonata, core and deseed the peppers, then finely slice them along with the onions and garlic. Heat 3 tablespoons of the olive oil in a large saucepan and fry the peppers, onions and garlic until they start to soften. Stir in the plum tomatoes, saffron and sugar or sweetener. Cook until soft and well combined, about 20–30 minutes, then add the basil and capers. Check the seasoning and set aside to keep warm. Preheat the oven to 200°C/400°F/gas 6.

Cut each chorizo sausage in half and thread on to the skewers with the cubes of monkfish. Brush all over with a little oil. Heat a griddle pan or heavy-based frying pan until very hot, then griddle or fry for a few minutes until the monkfish is golden. Put the kebabs on to a baking sheet and cook in the oven for 10 minutes. Serve the kebabs on top of the pepperonata. If you have any pepperonata left over, it is great served cold.

potted shrimp and crab salad

The flavour of potted shrimps is so English. Who says we have no regional cuisine? There are some fantastic recipes around and this one reminds me of trips to the seaside at Lyme Regis. Sitting on the beach front with some potted shrimps, fresh crab and a white wine spritzer is a great way to lunch. You can buy small, brown shrimps from your fishmonger.

SERVES 6

125g/4oz butter
2 shallots, finely chopped
½ tsp ground mace
½ tsp grated nutmeg
½ tsp ground allspice
400g/13oz shelled brown shrimps
400g/13oz picked fresh white (and a small bit
    of brown) crab meat
juice and grated zest of 1 lemon
2 dashes of Tabasco
1 tbsp finely chopped parsley
1 tbsp finely snipped chives
salt and freshly ground black pepper

TO SERVE
lemon wedges
rocket and watercress

Melt the butter and add the shallots. Fry for about 5 minutes, until translucent. Stir in the mace, nutmeg and allspice and continue to cook for 2 minutes.

In a large bowl, mix the shrimps and crab meat. Then add the lemon juice and zest, the Tabasco and the herbs. Pour in the butter-spice mix and stir well. Season with salt and pepper and serve immediately with lemon wedges and the salad leaves.

lime-and-ginger-marinated salmon with mango and avocado salsa

This dish is the one that I chose for my first live cooking appearance. I was so nervous, but it went okay in the end. I only had seven minutes to prepare and cook it – you can take your time!

SERVES 4
4 salmon fillets
2.5cm/1in piece of fresh root ginger, grated
grated zest and juice of 1 lime
1 tsp soy sauce
2 small butternut squash
olive oil

FOR THE MANGO AND AVOCADO SALSA
1 mango
2 avocados
½ small red onion
1 red chilli, deseeded and finely chopped
1 small garlic clove, crushed
small handful of chopped coriander
juice of ½ lemon
juice of about 2 limes
salt

Lay the salmon fillets in a shallow dish. Mix the ginger, lime zest and juice and the soy sauce and pour over the salmon. Leave to marinate while you get everything else ready. Preheat the oven to 190°C/375°F/gas 5.

Cut the squash into quarters, then peel them with a sharp knife. Scoop out the seeds. Brush the squash with some olive oil, season, then roast for about 25–30 minutes, or until the wedges are softened and golden, but still keep their shape.

Make the salsa. Chop the mango, avocados and red onion into roughly the same-sized cubes, about 1cm/½in. Mix with the chilli, garlic, coriander, lemon juice and lime juice to taste. Season with salt and set aside.

When the squash is almost cooked, heat a little olive oil in a frying pan. Place the salmon skin-side down and cook until golden brown, 3–4 minutes. Turn over and cook lightly for a couple more minutes. Serve the salmon on the squash wedges, with a lovely big dollop of the salsa.

delicious dinners

This chapter contains some slightly more complex high-protein dishes. As a rule it's best not to combine carbs and protein in the same meal, but this book is all about balance. Keeping a sense of what you are eating, and eating intelligently are far more important than being rigid in your choices. This book is not about trying to lose weight, but about sustaining a healthy body whilst enjoying your food as well.

As a professional chef, I do love using butter for many dishes, because its flavour is unbeatable. Again, balance is the key. I do, however, also love olive oil, which is packed with fantastic properties and is always the healthy choice.

ostrich steaks with cassis and blueberry sauce

Ostrich is one of the healthiest meats you can eat. It is very high in iron and protein and lower in fat than chicken – so tuck in! When I was a teenager, I lived in Australia and Indonesia for 6 months which had a huge influence on my passion for flavoursome food. The Aussies began eating ostrich far sooner than we did and this dish also works well with kangaroo – another very lean meat. Stir-fried broccoli with chilli and garlic (see page 138) makes a great accompaniment.

SERVES 4
splash of olive oil
4 ostrich steaks, about 175g/6oz each
1 bottle reasonably good red wine
100ml/3½fl oz cassis (blackcurrant liqueur)
150g/5oz blueberries
¾ tsp cornflour
salt and freshly ground black pepper

Heat a large frying pan until very hot and add the olive oil. Add the steaks and seal them for 2 minutes on each side. Take the steaks out of the pan and put them on a baking sheet. Preheat the oven to 200°C/400°/gas 6.

Pour the wine into the remaining juices in the frying pan and reduce by half. Add the cassis and blueberries and continue reducing for a further 15 minutes.

Meanwhile, put the steaks in the oven for 10 minutes, or until the meat is cooked but still pink in the centre.

While the steaks are cooking, blend the cornflour with 2 teaspoons water until smooth. Stir this into the reduced sauce, and stir for a minute or two to thicken, then season to taste. Serve the steaks with the sauce puddled around them.

braised cinnamon rabbit

This dish has such warming flavours; the cinnamon really brings out the meaty depth of flavour in the rabbit. The dish is Greek in origin and tastes fantastic in summer or winter.

SERVES 4

200g/7oz baby (pickling) onions
1 rabbit, cut into portions (ask your butcher to help with this)
salt and freshly ground black pepper
splash of olive oil
2 garlic cloves
1 bay leaf
1 rosemary sprig or 1 tsp dried rosemary
1 rounded tsp ground cinnamon
½ bottle red wine
300ml/½ pint chicken stock (see page 180)
2 x 400g/13oz cans tomatoes
1 tsp Splenda sweetener

Peel the baby onions and season the rabbit portions with salt and pepper.

Heat a splash of olive oil in a large frying pan or saucepan, add the rabbit portions and fry until golden brown all over. Remove from the pan and set aside.

Fry the onions in the same pan until golden brown, adding more oil if necessary, then add the garlic, herbs and cinnamon. Return the rabbit to the pan and pour in the wine. Simmer for about 10 minutes to cook off the alcohol, then pour in the stock, tip in the tomatoes and add the sweetener. Bring to the boil, turn the heat down, cover and simmer gently for about 1¾ hours or until the meat is very tender.

moroccan chicken bake

Someone once said that a lot of my food is yellow! I do love colourful food that brings a bit of sunshine to our generally grey climate. Yellow and orange foods are also full of the antioxidant beta-carotene, so veg. such as squash, yellow peppers and carrots are very healthy and full of anti-cancer agents. The body also converts beta-carotene into vitamin E.

SERVES 4

2 tsp ground cumin
2 tsp ground coriander
½ tsp ground turmeric
1 tsp ground cinnamon
½ tsp saffron threads
3 cardamon pods, seeds removed and crushed
2 garlic cloves, crushed
2 red chillies, deseeded and finely chopped
splash of olive oil
4 skinless, boneless chicken breasts, preferably
    free-range
1 butternut squash
2 red onions
1 orange, peel left on
225g/8oz ready-to-eat dried apricots
salt and freshly ground black pepper
handful of fresh coriander
handful of fresh mint

Mix all the spices together with the garlic and chillies. Stir in the olive oil and divide the mixture between 2 bowls.

Add the chicken breasts to 1 of the bowls and rub in the spice mixture. Heat a frying pan until it is very hot and brown off the chicken breasts until golden all over, but do not cook them. Remove from the pan and set aside. Preheat the oven to 200°C/400°F/gas 6.

Cut the squash into quarters, then peel off the skin with a sharp knife and scoop out the seeds. Cut the squash and onions into wedges and the orange into chunks, then tip them, along with the apricots, into the other bowl containing the spice mix and toss well.

Put the vegetable and apricot mix on to a baking sheet, season and bake for 20 minutes. Place the browned chicken pieces on top of the vegetables and return to the oven to cook for a further 15–20 minutes, or until everything is tender.

Whilst this is finishing, roughly chop the coriander and mint. Just before serving, sprinkle the herbs over the chicken bake.

smoked mozzarella wrapped in pancetta

Smoked mozzarella is fantastic grilled. In this recipe the smoky flavour combines perfectly with the balsamic onions. Serve with a big green salad and you're ready to go.

SERVES 4
12 baby (pickling) onions
2 heads of radicchio
splash of olive oil
3 tbsp balsamic vinegar
leaves from 1 rosemary sprig
2 whole smoked mozzarella cheeses
8 slices of pancetta

Peel the baby onions, then cook in boiling water for about 3–4 minutes to blanch. Drain and pat dry with kitchen paper. Halve each radicchio. Heat the olive oil in a frying pan, tip in the onions and cook until they are browned and cooked through (but not burnt), turning often.

Add the radicchio, balsamic vinegar and rosemary leaves and cook until there is only 1 tablespoon of the liquid left. Keep warm.

Cut each mozzarella into quarters, then wrap each piece in a slice of pancetta. Heat a griddle pan or heavy-based frying pan and put the mozzarella on the griddle or in the frying pan, with the join of the pancetta underneath. Cook quickly to lightly brown each side, but not too long or the mozzarella will melt too much. Serve 2 quarters of mozzarella, half a radicchio and 3 baby onions per plate.

pan-roasted halibut with oyster, bacon and cabbage fricassée

Sometimes fish dishes can seem too light, but this one, with a mix of halibut and oysters, is really good and hearty. Oysters are reputed to be an aphrodisiac because of their high levels of zinc, which enhances male fertility. Aside from that, they are also very low in fat and high in vitamins and minerals. Just be careful how much champagne you knock back with them!

SERVES 4
8 oysters
½ Savoy cabbage
3 smoked streaky bacon rashers
25g/1oz butter
1 onion, finely sliced
2 garlic cloves, crushed
125ml/4fl oz white wine
1 thyme sprig
100ml/3½fl oz double cream
salt and freshly ground black pepper
splash of olive oil
4 halibut steaks, on the bone

First, shuck the oysters (see page 187), reserving the oyster meat and juices. Then prepare the cabbage and bacon. Cut the cabbage into quarters and discard the hard core. Chop the quarters into rough chunks and cut the bacon into lardons (small pieces).

Heat the butter in a large saucepan and fry the bacon and onion for 4–5 minutes, until starting to turn golden. Add the garlic and cook for another minute. Turn up the heat and add the cabbage and white wine. Stir, then put the lid on to semi-steam the cabbage, checking occasionally to make sure it doesn't burn, for about 5–8 minutes. Add the thyme and cream and reduce the liquid until it is of a sauce consistency, about 4–5 minutes. The cabbage should be cooked, but still have some bite. When the sauce and cabbage are just right, remove from the heat, taste and season if necessary. Set aside.

Heat a frying pan, add a splash of oil and cook the halibut, skin-side down, until golden, about 3–4 minutes. Turn the fish over and cook the other side for about 3 more minutes until done. Add the oysters and their juice to the cabbage and gently warm through (you just want to warm the oysters). To serve, pile the cabbage mix in the middle of each plate and sit the halibut on top.

the very best roast chicken

You may not think this is the most inspiring recipe, but I really do love a good roast chicken. It's comfort food *extraordinaire*, but it doesn't have to be unhealthy. Eating this always takes me right back to being at home with my family, so if I'm feeling ill or down, I always cook a chicken. As an accompaniment to my version, try Spiced red cabbage (see page 132), or Stir-fried broccoli with chilli and garlic (see page 138).

SERVES 4
1 lemon
1 onion
1 x 1.8–2kg/4–4½lb free-range or organic chicken
1 whole garlic bulb
1 small bunch each of thyme, rosemary and sage
1 tbsp olive oil
salt and freshly ground black pepper

Preheat the oven to 220°C/425°F/gas 7. Finely grate the zest from half of the lemon and reserve, then cut the lemon and onion in half and place inside the chicken cavity. Crush the garlic bulb so the cloves separate, and distribute them in the cavity, between the legs and around the chicken, keeping 1 clove back.

Tuck the thyme and rosemary inside the cavity of the chicken. Chop the sage leaves and the remaining garlic clove. Mix the chopped sage with the olive oil, the lemon zest, the chopped garlic and some salt and pepper. Carefully ease the skin from the breast of the chicken, being careful not to tear it, then rub the sage mixture between the skin and the flesh. Put the chicken in a roasting tin.

Season the chicken all over and roast for 20 minutes, then lower the oven temperature to 190°C/375°F/gas 5, turn the chicken over so it is breast-side down, and roast for a further 30 minutes. Turn the chicken breast-side up again and roast for another 30 minutes, or until cooked through.

Remove the chicken from the oven, cover loosely with foil and leave to rest for 10 minutes before serving.

turkey, pistachio and apricot roulade with orange sauce

You don't need to save turkey for Christmas. It's a really healthy white meat, lower in fat than chicken and easily digested.

SERVES 4
8 turkey escalopes, about 125g/4oz each
butter and olive oil, for frying

FOR THE STUFFING
1 onion
2 garlic cloves
splash of olive oil
225g/8oz ready-to-eat dried apricots
125g/4oz pistachios
50g/2oz ground almonds
salt and freshly ground black pepper
1 egg, beaten

FOR THE ORANGE SAUCE
500ml/17fl oz orange juice
200ml/7fl oz white wine
25g/1oz butter
1 tbsp finely chopped flat-leaf parsley

Make the stuffing. Finely chop the onion and garlic, heat a splash of oil in a frying pan and fry them until softened but not brown. Chop the apricots and blitz the pistachios in a blender until semi-fine. Stir the apricots, pistachios and ground almonds into the onion and garlic. Season, then mix in the beaten egg.

Lay the escalopes on a board and, if they are thick, beat them with a meat mallet, or put them between 2 sheets of parchment paper and beat with a rolling pin. Put about 2 teaspoons of the stuffing mixture in a sausage-shape down the middle of each escalope. Roll them up tightly and secure each one with 3 cocktail sticks.

Heat a frying pan, add a knob of butter and a splash of olive oil and fry the escalopes briefly over a high heat until golden brown on both sides, about 4 minutes. Set aside.

Put all the sauce ingredients, except the parsley, in a large, wide saucepan and heat until the butter has melted. Add the turkey roulades and simmer for 20 minutes, turning them in the sauce occasionally. Lift the escalopes from the sauce with a slotted spoon and keep them warm and covered. Bubble the sauce until it is reduced by about two thirds to a shiny orange glaze, about 10–15 minutes. Season and add the parsley.

Slice each roulade to serve, allowing 2 per plate, and pour the sauce over.

sliced teriyaki steak
with cucumber relish

Before I visited Japan for the first time, someone told me that it is completely different from the West in every way and it was! I've travelled all over the world, but I think Japan has the most contrasts. I found the taste of the food unusual and unexpected, and loved the way it left you feeling refreshed because of all the lovely clean flavours. This dish is great with some stir-fried garlicky greens.

SERVES 4

4 sirloin steaks, preferably organic
splash of olive oil
wasabi (Japanese horseradish), to serve

FOR THE MARINADE

3 tbsp teriyaki sauce
1 tbsp sweet soy sauce
1 tbsp soy sauce
2 garlic cloves, crushed

FOR THE CUCUMBER RELISH

1½–2 cucumbers, depending on your appetite
2 tsp salt
300ml/½ pint white rice vinegar
1 tbsp sugar or 1 tsp Splenda sweetener

Mix all the marinade ingredients together in a glass dish, add the steaks and leave them to marinate for an hour or so, or overnight.

For the relish, peel and deseed the cucumbers. Slice them in half lengthways through the middle, scoop out the watery seeds, then cut the flesh into very thin diagonal slices. Put the slices in a shallow dish, sprinkle them with the salt and leave for 20 minutes. Tip them into a colander or large sieve and put under running cold water to rinse off the salt. Drain very well and tip into a dish. Heat the rice vinegar and sugar or sweetener in a small saucepan until the latter has dissolved, then pour the mixture over the cucumber. Chill.

When ready to serve, heat a frying pan until very hot, pour in a splash of olive oil, and fry the steaks for 3–4 minutes on each side, but keep them quite rare. Leave them to rest for 10 minutes, then slice on to serving plates. Serve with the cucumber relish and some wasabi, and a side dish of your choice.

spiced swordfish with sweetcorn and sweet pepper salsa

When my clients want a healthy Mexican dish, this is always a favourite. It has lots of flavour, yet is filled with good fats and vegetables. It's also delicious made with spiced chicken breasts instead of the swordfish, and some refried beans.

SERVES 4
4 swordfish steaks
splash of olive oil
lime wedges, to serve

FOR THE SWORDFISH SPICE MIX
½ tsp ground cumin
½ tsp ground coriander
½ tsp paprika
½ tsp dried oregano
¼ tsp ground turmeric
½ tsp garlic salt
2 tbsp olive oil
pinch of freshly ground black pepper

FOR THE SALSA
1 red pepper
1–2 red chillies (depending how hot you like it)
1 red onion
½ small garlic clove
½ bunch of coriander
250g/8½oz sweetcorn, off the cob (fresh, frozen or canned)
2 tbsp olive oil
juice of 1 lime

FOR THE GUACAMOLE
3 ripe avocados, peeled and stoned
½ small garlic clove
juice of 2 limes

Combine all the ingredients for the spice mix. Lay the swordfish in a shallow dish and spread the spice mix over to cover. Leave to marinate for 20 minutes.

For the salsa, deseed and finely chop the pepper and chilli. Finely chop the onion, garlic and coriander. Mix with the sweetcorn, olive oil and lime juice.

For the guacamole, blitz the avocados, garlic and lime juice together until smooth (or mash with a fork if you like a bit more texture). Season to taste.

Heat a frying pan, add a splash of olive oil and fry the swordfish steaks for about 2–3 minutes on each side. I like mine quite rare, but cook them to your personal taste. Serve with lime wedges, the salsa and the guacamole.

sea bass and braised leeks with clam and herb dressing

This goes very well with the Pernod braised fennel (see page 130). It uses a lot of herbs which give flavour without adding calories. People should really get into the habit of using them more!

SERVES 4

1kg/2lb clams, in their shells
200ml/7fl oz white wine
2 shallots, finely chopped
3 tbsp olive oil
grated zest and juice of 2 lemons
1 tbsp snipped chives
1 tbsp chopped flat-leaf parsley
1 tbsp chopped tarragon
salt and freshly ground black pepper
4 large leeks
750ml/1¼ pints vegetable stock
1 bay leaf
4 sea bass fillets, cut in half lengthways

Heat a large saucepan until very hot. Tip in the clams and white wine and cover. When the shells have steamed open, remove and discard any that are still closed. Remove the clams from the pan, reserving the liquid, and pick out all the clam meat, discarding the shells.

In a separate saucepan, lightly fry the shallots in 2 tablespoons of the olive oil until softened but not brown. Add the clam cooking liquid, the lemon zest and juice and all the herbs except the bay leaf. Remove from the heat, check the seasoning and add the clam meat. Set aside.

Trim the leeks and cut each into 4 equal pieces. Pour the stock into a deep frying pan, add the bay leaf and bring to the boil. Add the leeks and simmer for 20 minutes, or until cooked.

When the leeks are nearly cooked, heat another frying pan, pour in the rest of the oil and fry the sea bass, skin-side down, for 2–3 minutes until golden brown. Turn the fish over and cook the flesh side for a minute or two.

To serve, return the saucepan of clam dressing to the heat and gently warm through. Remove the leeks from the pan with a slotted spoon and put 4 pieces on each plate. Arrange the sea bass on top and surround with the clam dressing.

rolled stuffed pork fillet wrapped in parma ham

Pork fillet is a cheap cut of meat, but a tender one. Using frozen peas and beans means you can serve this at any time, but use fresh when they are in season. The combination of the peas and beans goes really well with tangy pecorino cheese. If you want this dish to look especially smart for a dinner party, and you have the time, peel the skins off the broad beans after they have thawed.

SERVES 4

2 garlic cloves, finely chopped
1 tbsp finely chopped sage
1 tbsp finely chopped parsley
1 tsp wholegrain (Meaux) mustard
4 tbsp olive oil
salt and freshly ground black pepper
2 pork fillets, about 450–500g/14½oz–1lb
    each
8 slices of Parma ham or prosciutto
300g/10oz frozen broad beans, thawed
    (skins removed, optional)
300g/10oz frozen petits pois, thawed
juice of 1 lemon
1 tbsp chopped mint
shavings of pecorino cheese, to serve

Preheat the oven to 190°C/375°F/gas 5. Mix the garlic with the sage and parsley, the mustard and 1 tablespoon of the olive oil. Season.

Trim off any sinew and fat from the pork fillets. Cut a lengthways slit half-way through each pork fillet to make a pocket. Fill the pocket with some of the herb and mustard mixture, and rub it on the outside of the fillets as well. Wrap each fillet neatly in the Parma ham or prosciutto to cover it completely, using 4 slices per fillet (this usually depends on how long the fillet is, but 3–4 is usual). Cut each fillet in half to make 4 pieces.

Heat a large frying pan, pour in another tablespoon of the oil, add the wrapped pork fillets and cook until they are lightly browned all over, turning occasionally. Place them on a baking sheet and roast for 10 minutes until cooked.

While the pork is roasting, very gently heat the beans and peas in a saucepan with the lemon juice and the rest of the olive oil. Season and scatter in the mint. Slice each piece of pork fillet and serve with the beans and peas, and a scattering of pecorino shavings.

calf's liver with caramelised onions on parsnip bubble and squeak

This dish is a great winter warmer. Parsnips do have a high glycaemic index, though, as they're a starchy vegetable, so this isn't a dish to eat every day.

SERVES 4

300g/10oz grapes
2–3 tbsp olive oil
700g/1½lb calf's liver, trimmed, cleaned and
    thinly sliced

FOR THE BUBBLE AND SQUEAK
5 parsnips, cored and chopped
1 carrot, thinly sliced
2 tbsp olive oil
1 onion, roughly chopped
¼ spring cabbage, thinly sliced
salt and freshly ground black pepper
1 egg, beaten
flour, preferably wholemeal,
    for dusting

FOR THE CARAMELISED ONIONS
125g/4oz butter
4 onions, finely sliced
1 tsp chopped sage
2–3 tbsp balsamic vinegar

First, peel the grapes. I know this sounds ridiculous, and, of course, you don't have to, but they do look prettier and it can feel quite therapeutic to do (it's easier if you pour some warm water over the grapes first). Set aside.

For the bubble and squeak, put a pan of water on to boil, add the parsnips and simmer, covered, for 15 minutes. Add the carrot and continue cooking for another 10 minutes. Drain well, then crush with a fork or potato masher and set aside. Heat the oil in a large frying pan and fry the onion and cabbage until softened. Stir in the crushed parsnips and carrot. Season and mix in the egg. Divide the mixture into 4, shape into patties and lightly dust with flour.

Make the caramelised onions. Melt the butter in a large frying pan, tip in the onions and sage and cook on a low heat for about 20–25 minutes, until the onions are very soft and golden. Stir in the balsamic vinegar to taste, and cook until everything is caramelised. Add the grapes and keep warm.

In a large, non-stick frying pan, heat 1 tablespoon oil, and fry the patties on both sides until golden brown. Keep warm.

Wipe out the pan, heat a splash of olive oil and quickly fry the liver for about 3 minutes on each side. The timing depends on the thickness of the liver, but keep it nice and pink inside.

Serve the liver on the bubble and squeak patties, with the caramelised onions and grapes.

venison with pink peppercorn crust and celeriac mash

Game meats such as venison are a good replacement for beef and a bit more exciting. Higher in iron and lower in fat, they also have a more intense flavour. You can use the celeriac mash to accompany any meat dish and it's a good substitute for potatoes.

SERVES 4

125g/4oz mix of pink and green peppercorns
    in brine, drained
2 medium celeriacs
milk
50g/2oz butter
salt and freshly ground black pepper
4 venison leg steaks
splash of olive oil
5 tbsp brandy
200ml/7fl oz beef stock
green salad, to serve

Tip the peppercorns into a bowl and crush them using the base of a rolling pin (or use a pestle and mortar). Set aside. Peel the celeriacs and cut them into medium-sized chunks. Put them into a saucepan and pour in enough milk and water (equal quantities) to cover. Season with salt and bring to the boil. Lower the heat and simmer, covered, for 20 minutes or until tender. Drain well, mash with half the butter and season to taste. Preheat the oven to 180°C/350°F/gas 4.

Season the venison steaks with salt and black pepper. Heat a frying pan, add a splash of oil and fry the steaks for 2 minutes on each side. Take them out of the pan and lay them on a baking sheet. Pat a thin layer of the crushed peppercorns on to each venison steak and roast for about 8–12 minutes. The cooking time is approximate as it depends on the thickness of the steaks, but they must be served pink in the middle.

Meanwhile, pour the brandy carefully into the frying pan as it should catch light and *flambé*, and deglaze the pan by scraping the sediment from the bottom. Add the beef stock and let the mixture bubble away until it has reduced by half (about 15 minutes). Cut the rest of the butter into small pieces and add to the pan bit by bit, stirring as you do so, to make a glossy gravy. Season to taste.

Serve with a green salad, a big dollop of celeriac mash and the brandy gravy.

lentil, pear and smoked duck salad

Filling and sustaining, lentils are high in fibre and rich in valuable nutrients, as well as being a source of protein. The French have turned the humble lentil into a gastro-ingredient and Puy lentils are my favourite for this recipe.

SERVES 4

300g/10oz Puy lentils
1 litre/1¾ pints chicken stock (see page 180)
225g/8oz peeled whole vacuum-packed
    chestnuts
1 red onion, finely chopped
1 tbsp balsamic vinegar
1 tbsp olive oil, plus extra for drizzling
1 tbsp wholegrain mustard
2 tbsp finely chopped flat-leaf parsley
salt and freshly ground black pepper
3 smoked duck breasts
2 pears
125g/4oz rocket

Put the lentils and stock into a saucepan and bring to the boil. Simmer, covered, for about 25 minutes, or until the lentils are just cooked and still keeping their shape. Drain the lentils and tip into a mixing bowl.

Roughly chop the chestnuts and mix into the lentils with the onion, vinegar, olive oil, mustard, parsley and seasoning. Set aside.

Thinly slice the duck breasts. Core the pears (no need to peel) and thinly slice them too. To serve, scatter some rocket in the centre of each plate and drizzle with a little olive oil. Pile on some of the lentil mixture, then arrange the sliced duck and pears elegantly on top.

cider pot-roasted chicken

A lovely, heart-warming dish, where the cider gives the chicken masses of flavour. Serve with a couple of side dishes, such as Kohlrabi dauphinois (see page 123) and Ginger-glazed roasted beetroot (see page 131).

SERVES 4

50g/2oz butter
1 x 1.6–1.8kg/3½lb–4lb free-range or organic chicken
3 carrots
2 leeks
3 celery sticks
3 onions
2 garlic cloves
4 thyme sprigs
2 bay leaves
500ml/17fl oz good quality dry cider
500ml/17fl oz chicken stock (see page 180)
salt and freshly ground black pepper

Melt the butter in a saucepan that is large enough to take the chicken (and the vegetables later on). Sit the chicken in the pan, breast-side down, and fry until golden brown, about 5 minutes. Remove the chicken from the pan and set aside.

Cut the carrots into small pieces, then cut the leeks and celery to a similar size. Peel and chop the onions and roughly chop the garlic. Tip all the vegetables and the herbs into the pan and fry for about 8 minutes, stirring often.

Return the chicken to the pan and nestle it in between the vegetables. Pour in the cider and bring to the boil. Finally, add the stock and cover. Bring to the boil, then turn the heat down and simmer for 1–1½ hours, until the chicken is completely cooked. Taste and add seasoning if necessary.

veal escalopes with porcini

This is a very traditional Italian dish. I love porcini mushrooms – they are the most sexy, meaty and fabulous mushrooms ever, though they are quite difficult to get in England (autumn is the best time for them). In Italy, when they are in season, you see them everywhere, and I've been known to come back with a suitcase full of them. If you have trouble tracking them down, you can use a mix of wild mushrooms, or dried porcini instead. If using dried, soak in hot water for 1 hour previously.

SERVES 4

8 thin veal escalopes
salt and freshly ground black pepper
olive oil, for frying
2 garlic cloves
300g/10oz fresh porcini mushrooms (ceps),
    or any mix of wild mushrooms
200ml/7fl oz marsala wine
1½ tbsp crème fraîche
1 tbsp chopped flat-leaf parsley

Season the escalopes with salt and pepper, then heat a splash of oil in a frying pan and fry the escalopes for 2 minutes on each side. Lift them out of the pan and leave them to rest on a plate, covered, while you make the sauce.

Finely chop the garlic and slice the porcini. Add another generous splash of olive oil to the pan, tip in the mushrooms and garlic and fry until soft. Pour in the marsala, bring to the boil, then let it bubble until reduced by half, about 5–8 minutes. Stir in the crème fraîche and the parsley, along with any juices that have collected from the meat, and continue to reduce until it's of a good sauce consistency. Return the meat to the sauce briefly to warm through, then season and serve.

steamed seabass with ginger and bok choi

This recipe is for one of those days when you feel you've been over-indulging. Too many canapés and champagne can all take their toll and sometimes you need some purist food. This is it.

SERVES 2

2.5cm/1in piece of fresh root ginger
1 red chilli
4 spring onions
1 large sea bass, weighing about 1kg/2lb, cleaned
juice of 1 lime
salt and freshly ground black pepper
3 heads of bok choi
1 garlic clove
splash of vegetable oil
few drops of sesame oil
3 tbsp soy sauce
lime wedges, to serve

Cut the ginger into fine strips. Deseed the chilli and cut it into fine strips. Roughly chop the spring onions and mix with the ginger and chilli.

Make several diagonal slashes in the skin of the sea bass with a sharp knife. Fill the slits and the cavity of the fish with the ginger, chilli and spring onions.

Put the sea bass in a steamer. Squeeze over the juice of the lime and season with salt and pepper. Steam for 20–25 minutes, or until cooked. (Alternatively, sit the fish on a large sheet of foil, squeeze over the lime, season, then loosely wrap the foil around the fish to make a parcel and bake in the oven at 200°C/400°F/gas 6 for 30 minutes.)

While the fish is cooking, roughly chop the bok choi and slice the garlic. Heat both the oils in a wok and fry the garlic briefly. Add the bok choi and stir-fry for 3 minutes, then pour in the soy sauce and cook for another minute or two, or until the bok choi is tender but still has a crunch to it.

Serve the sea bass with the bok choi and lime wedges for squeezing over.

rack of lamb
with caponata and herb oil

Caponata is Sicilian in origin and has an almost sweet and sour flavour. This cuts through the richness of the lamb perfectly. Caponata is also great served cold with sliced meats and cheeses.

SERVES 4

2 aubergines

2 onions

1 red pepper, deseeded

3–4 tbsp olive oil

½ tsp dried oregano

3 tbsp white wine

400g/13oz can tomatoes

1 tsp balsamic vinegar

1 tbsp torn basil

50g/2oz capers, rinsed

2 large racks of lamb (usually a rack has 8 bones, so cut them in half and you will have 4 portions with 4 bones in each; each portion should weigh about 250g/8½oz)

FOR THE HERB OIL

1 tbsp basil leaves

1 tbsp parsley leaves

1 tbsp mint leaves

150ml/¼ pint extra-virgin olive oil

salt and freshly ground black pepper

First, to make the herb oil, blitz the herbs and oil together in a small food processor until the herbs are very fine, then season well. Set aside.

Make the caponata. Dice the aubergines, onions and red pepper into small squares. Heat 2–3 tablespoons of the olive oil in a frying pan and fry the vegetables together until starting to soften.

Add the oregano and white wine, and allow to cook for a minute or two until the wine is reduced by half. Tip in the tomatoes, then the balsamic vinegar. Cook gently, uncovered, for about 30 minutes to make a rich sauce, stirring occasionally. Stir in the torn basil and capers at the end. Preheat the oven to 200°C/400°F/gas 6.

While the caponata is simmering, trim any surplus fat from the lamb. Heat another table-spoon of the olive oil and fry the lamb until golden on both sides, about 4 minutes. Put the lamb in a roasting tin and roast for 10–15 minutes. This is for medium-rare, so cook for a bit longer if you like it well done. Remove from the oven and let it rest for 5 minutes, covered.

Serve the rack of lamb with a good dollop of caponata and a drizzle of the herb oil.

slow-roasted pork
with sage and apple butter

My family lives in Somerset, and whenever I go home we visit a local organic farm shop at Pitney Farm. They have the most adorable little free-range pigs. Cute though they are, they do grow up into delicious organic pork. As you'll discover, organic pork is a world away from the sugar-, salt- and water-injected stuff at the supermarket. So try to source it from a good supplier.

SERVES 6

1 leg of pork, preferably organic
    weighing about 2.5kg/5½lb
salt and freshly ground black pepper
4 parsnips
5 carrots
2 turnips
3 beetroot
3 red onions
6 garlic cloves

FOR THE SAGE AND APPLE BUTTER
3 cooking apples
2 shallots
¼ bunch of sage
125g/4oz butter
1½ tbsp cider vinegar
1 tsp light muscovado sugar

Preheat the oven to 160°C/325°F/gas 3. Sprinkle the pork lightly with salt, then rub it in all over. Lay the pork in a large roasting tin, cover loosely with foil and roast for 2½ hours. While the pork is roasting, core the parsnips and cut into large pieces, and chop the carrots, turnips, beetroot and onions into similar-sized pieces and peel the garlic. After the pork has roasted for 2½ hours, remove the foil and turn the oven up to 200°C/400°F/gas 6. Scatter all the vegetables and the garlic around the pork, turn them in the meat juices to coat, season them, then put everything in the oven for another hour.

While the pork and vegetables finish cooking, make the sage and apple butter. Peel, core and dice the apples. Finely chop the shallots and sage. Melt the butter in a saucepan and fry the shallots for 2–3 minutes. Tip in the apples and fry them for another couple of minutes, then add the sage, cider vinegar and sugar. Cook right down to a fresh chutney-like state. This should take about 10 minutes.

Slice the pork and serve with the roasted vegetables and sage and apple butter.

black-pepper stir-fried crab

I first ate this in an amazing beach-side shack-cum-restaurant in Malaysia. The restaurant's food was completely eclectic, with Chinese, Indian and Malaysian styles all mixed together, and the seafood was out of this world. This is a very messy dish to eat – I love it! I usually serve it as part of a Malay feast where everyone just digs in and helps themselves.

SERVES 2

2 tbsp black peppercorns
5 spring onions
3 crabs, preferably blue swimmer
1 tbsp vegetable oil
4 garlic cloves, finely chopped
2 tbsp soy sauce
1 tbsp Thai fish sauce
2 whole dried chillies
3 tbsp sweet soy sauce (Malaysian)
salt (optional)

In a small electric blender, roughly crush the peppercorns (or use a pestle and mortar). Roughly chop the spring onions. Set both aside.

Split the crabs in half down the centre cavity with a sharp knife. Heat the oil in a saucepan and add the garlic. Next add the peppercorns and crabs and stir-fry for 5–6 minutes. Pour in the soy sauce and fish sauce, then cover with a lid and cook for 10 minutes, stirring occasionally.

Take off the lid and tip in the dried chillies, spring onions and sweet soy sauce. Continue cooking for a couple of minutes, then check to see if any salt is needed. Serve on a platter.

seared lemon and fennel tuna with marinated fennel shavings

Tuna can dry out very quickly, so be careful not to overcook it. It's packed with omega-3 fish oils, great for your joints.

SERVES 4
2 fennel bulbs
1 red chilli
1 garlic clove
3 lemons
3 tbsp olive oil
salt and freshly ground black pepper
225g/8oz cherry tomatoes
1 tbsp chopped basil
4 tuna steaks
1 tsp fennel seeds

Slice the fennel very thinly using a mandolin if you have one, otherwise a very sharp knife. Deseed and finely chop the chilli and chop the garlic. Mix together the fennel, chilli and garlic. Squeeze in the juice of 2 of the lemons and pour in 2 tablespoons of the olive oil. Season, stir and leave to marinate for 1 hour.

After the hour, halve the tomatoes and add to the fennel with the basil.

Rub the tuna steaks all over with the fennel seeds and some salt and pepper. Drizzle with the rest of the olive oil. Fry the tuna in a hot pan for 2 minutes on each side. Remove the fish from the pan, put on serving plates and squeeze over the juice from the remaining lemon. Serve the tuna with the marinated fennel.

grilled lobster with brandy and herbs

It's a cliché, but lobster is wonderful and it tastes great combined with the flavours of brandy, herbs, garlic and butter. All you need is a simple green salad to serve with it.

SERVES 4

2 tbsp olive oil
125g/4oz butter
250g/8½oz cherry tomatoes
4 garlic cloves, finely chopped
1 rosemary sprig
100ml/3½fl oz brandy
2 tbsp white wine
salt and freshly ground black pepper
4 medium lobsters, about 1kg/2lb each,
　　cooked
3 tbsp chopped flat-leaf parsley
green salad, to serve

Heat a frying pan. Add the olive oil, butter, tomatoes, garlic and rosemary to the pan and cook for 2–3 minutes. Pour in the brandy and wine and cook everything for a further 8–10 minutes or until the tomatoes have softened slightly but still retain their shape. Season to taste.

Preheat the grill to high. On a large chopping board, take a large, sharp, chef's knife and cut the lobsters between the eyes. Then cut them right down the middle and completely in half. Put the lobsters in a roasting tin, cut-side up, and pour the tomato sauce over them. Grill for about 5 minutes until heated through.

Serve sprinkled with parsley and with a green salad on the side.

can-do carbs

I have included this chapter because sometimes you want the option of having a healthy carbohydrate fix. While I recommend eating these dishes only for lunch, not dinner, and only instead of a high-protein meal, it really is up to you.

The following recipes contain a high level of complex carbohydrates and a tiny amount of protein, if any. Try not to mix these carb dishes with any of the protein-based dishes or side orders at the same meal, as proteins and carbs are better digested separately.

wholewheat penne with roast butternut squash

My love of pasta grew when I had an Italian boyfriend for three years and spent a lot of time with him in Italy. We both shared an amazing passion for food, and he taught me a great deal about Italian cuisine. I love the Italian emphasis on the social side of eating and, of course, they know how to make fantastic food. The only down-side is that the Italian diet contains a lot of refined carbs, and I used to find myself feeling tired and bloated after a few weeks there. Wholemeal pasta has a lower glycaemic index than white, releasing sugar more slowly into the bloodstream. It's much better for you and provides sustained energy over a longer period.

SERVES 4

1 butternut squash
4 tbsp olive oil, plus extra for drizzling
salt and freshly ground black pepper
½ tsp dried chilli flakes
400g/13oz wholewheat penne
1 medium head of broccoli
2 garlic cloves
1 tbsp chopped sage
chilli oil (see page 183), optional

Preheat the oven to 200°C/400°F/gas 6. Cut the squash into quarters, then scoop out the seeds and cut off the skin with a sharp knife. Cut the squash into cubes. Scatter the squash on a baking sheet, drizzle with 3 tablespoons of the olive oil, toss together and season. Sprinkle with the chilli flakes and roast for 20–30 minutes or until tender.

Put a large pan of salted water on to boil. When the squash is cooked, add the pasta to the boiling water. Cook for 5 minutes.

Meanwhile, cut the broccoli into florets, then add it to the pasta water and continue cooking until the pasta is cooked, about another 10 minutes. I wouldn't normally cook broccoli this long, but it almost makes a sauce when the florets break up. Drain the pasta and broccoli in a colander.

Roughly chop the garlic and fry in the remaining olive oil in the pan the pasta was cooked in. Tip the pasta and broccoli back into the pan and add the roast squash. Add the sage, season, stir together and serve drizzled with extra olive oil, or chilli oil.

brown rice, peanut and carrot salad

Eating this salad makes me feel very virtuous. My childhood diet included a lot of wholefoods. White bread, margarine and jam sandwiches were a mysterious alien pleasure which other children experienced, not me. As a result, I have to say that I went through a phase of completely slating the wholefood idea – and used to call it 'lentil torture'. Now though, I'm realising the benefits of a no-sugar, wholefood diet and apologise to my Mum for giving her so much grief!

SERVES 4

250g/8½oz brown rice, preferably organic
1 red onion
5 carrots
125g/4oz roasted peanuts
1 tbsp chopped coriander
juice of 1 lemon
2 tbsp soy sauce
dash of Tabasco
splash of olive oil
splash of sesame oil
salt and freshly ground black pepper

Cook the rice according to the packet instructions, as brown rice varies considerably. When it is cooked, drain well, tip into a bowl and leave to cool.

Finely chop the onion and coarsely grate the carrots. Coarsely chop the peanuts and mix everything in with the rice. Stir in the coriander, lemon juice, soy sauce, Tabasco, olive oil and sesame oil, taste and adjust the salt and pepper, if necessary.

saffron and lemon brown rice pilau

For this pilau, fluffy, nutty grains of rice are scented with lemon and saffron. When you need some comfort carbs, this really hits the spot.

SERVES 4
1 fennel bulb
1 onion
2 garlic cloves
2 tbsp olive oil
3 cardamom pods, lightly crushed
½ tsp fennel seeds
250g/8½oz brown rice, preferably organic
500–750ml/17fl oz–1¼ pints vegetable stock
pinch of saffron threads
2 tbsp chopped parsley
2–3 tbsp lemon juice
salt and freshly ground black pepper

Finely chop the fennel, onion and garlic. Heat the oil in a medium saucepan and gently fry the fennel, onion and garlic until softened but not brown. Stir in the cardamom pods, fennel seeds and rice and continue cooking and stirring for a couple of minutes.

Pour in the stock, starting off with 500ml/17fl oz, add the saffron, then cover and cook for about 30 minutes or until all the stock is absorbed and the rice is just tender, adding more stock if necessary. When the rice is ready, take the pan off the heat, leave the lid on and let the rice rest for 5 minutes. This allows the steam to separate the rice grains. Stir in the parsley and lemon juice to taste, season and serve.

jewelled couscous

I call this 'jewelled' couscous, because when you cut the vegetables into little rounds (known as 'solferino'), they look like tiny coloured mounds of jewels. Of course, it's a bit fancy and time-consuming balling vegetables with a mini melon baller, but it's worth it. Add the pine nuts and sultanas and this really looks very pretty.

SERVES 4

2 carrots
2 courgettes
1 red pepper
1 yellow pepper
400ml/14fl oz vegetable stock
125g/4oz ready-to-eat dried apricots
250g/8½oz couscous
125g/4oz sultanas
5 spring onions
50g/2oz toasted pine nuts
1 tbsp chopped mint
1 tbsp chopped parsley
salt and freshly ground pepper
2–3 tbsp lemon juice
3 tbsp olive oil

Prepare the vegetables. Peel the carrots but not the courgettes. Cut the carrots and courgettes into small balls using a small melon baller. (You can cut any leftover bits of vegetables into dice, or just dice the whole vegetables instead of cutting them into balls if you're short on time.) Deseed the peppers and cut into small dice.

Bring the stock to the boil in a saucepan. Add the carrots and cook for 5 minutes, then add the courgettes and peppers and cook for a further 4 minutes. Chop the apricots the same size as the peppers and set aside.

Tip the couscous into a mixing bowl and pour in the stock and vegetables. Stir in the apricots and sultanas and cover lightly with clingfilm. Leave until all the stock has been absorbed, about 5 minutes.

Stir the couscous with a fork to break it up, then finely slice the spring onions and mix into the couscous with the pine nuts, mint and parsley. Season and dress with the lemon juice and olive oil.

bok choi, ginger and mangetout stir-fry with sesame wild rice

I only use basmati rice when it's mixed with wild rice, as this lowers the glycaemic index. It also adds a bit more colour and interest to the dish.

SERVES 4–6

250g/8½oz mix of wild and basmati rice
3 heads of bok choi
1 red pepper, deseeded
225g/8oz mangetout
3 spring onions
1cm/½in piece of fresh root ginger
2 garlic cloves
1 red chilli, deseeded
1 tbsp sesame seeds
½ tsp sesame oil
about 2 tbsp soy sauce
splash of corn or vegetable oil

Put the rice and 500ml/17fl oz water into a saucepan. Cover and cook for 20–30 minutes, or until all the liquid is absorbed and the rice is cooked. The timing really depends on the rice, as it can vary. Take the pan off the heat, leave the lid on and let the rice rest for 5 minutes. This allows the steam to separate the rice grains.

While the rice is cooking, prepare and cook the vegetables. Cut the bok choi into large pieces and the red pepper into strips. Slice the mangetout diagonally across. Cut the spring onions into large pieces and the ginger into thin strips. Crush the garlic, then finally slice the chilli into rings (use as much chilli as you can handle).

Lightly toast the sesame seeds in a small, dry pan, tossing the pan often so they don't burn. Stir them into the rice with the sesame oil and 1–2 teaspoons of the soy sauce. Keep warm.

Heat a wok to very hot, then add a splash of corn oil. Stir-fry the red pepper and mangetout first for about a minute, then add the ginger, garlic and chilli and stir-fry for a couple of minutes. Finally add the bok choi, spring onions and a splash of soy sauce (about 1 tablespoon) and cook for 2–3 minutes, until everything is tender-crisp. Serve immediately.

thai curried buckwheat noodles

You'll have some extra curry paste left over from this recipe, but I always think it's worth making a bit more than you need. The paste will keep in the fridge for up to a week and it's great for jazzing up soups, curries and stir-fries.

SERVES 4

FOR THE CURRY PASTE
1½ tsp coriander seeds
1 tsp fennel seeds
1 tsp cumin seeds
½ tsp black peppercorns
2 shallots
5 garlic cloves
2.5cm/1in piece of fresh root ginger
1 lemongrass stalk
3 red chillies, deseeded
small bunch of coriander
4 tbsp vegetable oil
1 tsp ground turmeric
1 tsp shrimp paste
finely grated zest of 1 lime (keep the juice for
    the noodles)

FOR THE NOODLES
3 shallots
1 aubergine
½ butternut squash
splash of vegetable oil
400ml/14fl oz can coconut milk
400g/13oz buckwheat noodles
150g/5oz sugar snap peas
juice of 1 lime
salt and freshly ground black pepper
1 red chilli, deseeded and sliced, to garnish
    (optional)

Make the curry paste first. Finely grind the coriander, fennel and cumin seeds with the peppercorns in a small blender. Very roughly chop the shallots, garlic, ginger, lemongrass and chillies. Add to the blender with the remaining curry paste ingredients and blitz until fine.

For the noodles, slice the shallots and chop the aubergine into cubes. Halve the piece of squash, scoop out the seeds, peel off the skin with a sharp knife and cut the flesh into cubes the same size as the aubergine. Heat a splash of oil in a large saucepan and lightly fry the shallots. Stir in 2 tablespoons of the curry paste and continue cooking until the aroma comes out, about 2–3 minutes. Add the aubergine and squash and continue to fry for 5 minutes. Finally, pour in the coconut milk and simmer, covered, for a further 20 minutes, until the vegetables are almost tender.

While that is cooking, bring a pan of water to the boil, add the noodles and cook according to the instructions on the packet. Tip them into a colander to drain off the water.

Add the sugar snap peas and the noodles to the coconut mix and continue cooking for another 5 minutes. Stir in the lime juice, season to taste and serve, garnished with slices of chilli if you like.

sweetcorn and buckwheat blinis with chilli salsa

These are great little pancakes which taste fantastic. You can make them smaller for canapés, topped with the salsa and soured cream, or make them bigger for a main course. The real Mexican tang from the jalapenos is cooled by the soured cream.

MAKES ABOUT 8 LARGE OR 16 SMALL
BLINIS

284g/10oz can sweetcorn, drained
1 tsp chopped pickled jalapeno chillies
2 eggs
2 tbsp buckwheat flour
salt and freshly ground black pepper
olive oil, for frying

FOR THE SOURED CREAM MIX
5 spring onions
200ml/7fl oz soured cream

FOR THE SALSA
4 large ripe tomatoes
½ red onion
1 red chilli, deseeded
1 tbsp chopped coriander

First prepare the soured cream mix. Finely slice the spring onions and stir into the soured cream, then chill. Dice the tomatoes for the salsa. Finely dice the onion and chilli and mix together with the coriander. Season and chill also.

Make the blinis. Mix the sweetcorn and the chopped pickled chillies. Separate the eggs, saving the whites in a clean mixing bowl and dropping the yolks in with the sweetcorn. Stir the flour and some seasoning into the sweetcorn. Whisk the egg whites into stiff peaks and gently fold into the sweetcorn batter. It should be quite thick.

Heat a frying pan, add a splash of olive oil and cook the blinis in batches, allowing 1 heaped tablespoon of the mixture per blini. Cook for 2–3 minutes, then turn over and cook the other side for another couple of minutes, until lightly browned. Keep the cooked blinis warm while you finish the rest, adding more oil as needed. Serve immediately with the soured cream and salsa.

seaweed and ginger rice cakes with carrot and cucumber salad

I made these up because it's a different way to serve rice and I find that people enjoy dipping tidbits into sauces. You'll note that the rice is cooked for slightly longer than usual. This is to release more starch from it, which helps to hold the cakes together.

SERVES 4

250g/8½oz mix of wild rice and basmati
5 nori seaweed sheets, cut into thin strips
1 egg, beaten
2.5cm/1in piece of fresh root ginger
1 red chilli, deseeded
3 spring onions
1 tsp sesame seeds
salt and freshly ground black pepper
splash of vegetable or corn oil

FOR THE SALAD

3 carrots
1 cucumber
150ml/¼ pint white rice vinegar
3 tbsp mirin (sweet rice wine)

FOR THE DIPPING SAUCE

4 tbsp soy sauce
1 tbsp mirin
1 tbsp finely chopped pickled (pink sushi) ginger, plus 2 tsp liquid from the jar
1 tsp wasabi (Japanese horseradish, optional)

First cook the rice according to the instructions on the packet, cooking for just a couple of minutes extra. This will soften the rice, making it easier to shape the cakes later. Stir in the strips of seaweed, remove from the heat, drain the rice under running cold water to cool quickly and set aside.

Mix the rice and egg together. Finely dice the ginger and chilli and finely slice the spring onions. Toast the sesame seeds in a small, dry pan, shaking often so they do not burn. Stir into the rice with the ginger, chilli and spring onions and season. Shape the rice mix into 8 smallish 'cakes'. Heat a splash of oil in a frying pan and fry each rice cake for a few minutes on each side until golden. Keep warm.

Shave the carrots for the salad into wide, fine lengthways strips with a vegetable peeler. Halve the cucumber lengthways and scoop out the seeds. Shave the cucumber the same way as the carrots and mix them together in a shallow dish. Pour the vinegar and mirin over.

Mix all the ingredients together for the dipping sauce and pour into a small serving dish. Serve the rice cakes with the salad and dipping sauce.

quinoa with moroccan apricots, courgettes and peppers

Quinoa is a little-known South American grain. It has a delicate flavour and texture and is a great replacement for rice. It's unique in that it is high in unsaturated fat and low in cholesterol. It's also high in protein and rich in other nutrients. Perfect for vegetarians needing to maintain their protein levels.

SERVES 4

175g/6oz butternut squash
1 aubergine
2 courgettes
1 red pepper, deseeded
1 yellow pepper, deseeded
2 red onions
2 garlic cloves
2cm/¾in piece of fresh root ginger
generous splash of olive oil
1 tsp ground cumin
1 tsp ground coriander
½ tsp ground turmeric
1 tsp ground cinnamon
pinch of saffron threads
125g/4oz ready-to-eat dried apricots
400g/13oz can chopped plum tomatoes
200ml/7fl oz vegetable stock
salt and freshly ground black pepper
250g/8½oz quinoa
1 tbsp chopped mint
2 tbsp chopped fresh coriander
50g/2oz pine nuts, toasted

Prepare the vegetables. Peel the skin from the squash with a sharp knife and scoop out the seeds. Cut the squash into large pieces, along with the aubergine, courgettes and red and yellow peppers. Finely chop the onions, garlic and ginger. Heat a large saucepan. Pour in a generous splash of oil and start frying the onions, garlic and ginger, until soft but not brown. Stir in the spices and continue frying for a couple of minutes, then add the rest of the vegetables and the apricots, and fry for 2–3 minutes, adding a splash more oil if needed.

Tip in the tomatoes and stock, bring to the boil, then turn down the heat and simmer, uncovered, for 30–40 minutes, or until the liquid has a sauce consistency and the vegetables are cooked. Season to taste.

Meanwhile, cook the quinoa as you would for rice, allowing twice as much water as quinoa, and simmering for about 10–12 minutes until all the water has evaporated. Stir in the mint, fresh coriander and toasted pine nuts, season and serve with the vegetables.

on the side

These recipes are designed to be served alongside any of the protein-based lunch and dinner choices. They are mainly vegetarian and quite often substantial enough to have by themselves – great if veggie friends are coming for dinner. They'll also make a good contribution to the 4–5 portions of fruit and veg. a day we should all be eating.

Next to most of the recipes I've made suggestions for the main courses that they complement, but feel free to mix and match. After all, it's you who'll be sitting down to dinner!

leeks with gorgonzola and prunes

The amazingly rich combination of leeks and Gorgonzola is softened by the sweetness of the prunes. It's the perfect accompaniment to either Slow-roasted pork (see page 101) or a traditional roast chicken (page 84).

SERVES 6

8 leeks
50g/2oz butter
125g/4oz dried prunes, stoned
4–5 tbsp white wine
150g/5oz Gorgonzola cheese
salt and freshly ground black pepper

Finely slice the leeks. Melt the butter in a large frying pan and fry the leeks for about 5–8 minutes until starting to soften, stirring occasionally so they don't burn.

Chop the prunes and stir into the leeks. Pour in the wine and let it cook until it has almost disappeared. Crumble in the gorgonzola, give everything a stir, check the seasoning and serve.

kohlrabi dauphinois

Dauphinois is a fantastically rich French potato dish. By replacing the potatoes with kohlrabi (or you could use celeriac), and using less butter and cream, you can keep the comfort value, but reduce the guilt factor. Using less butter and cream, however, does mean that this is a drier dauphinois than the classic recipe.

SERVES 4
2–3 kohlrabi, depending on their size
100m/3½fl oz double cream
100ml/3½fl oz milk
1 garlic clove, crushed
25g/2oz butter
pinch of freshly grated nutmeg
salt and freshly ground black pepper

Preheat the oven to 180°C/350°F/gas 4. Trim and peel the kohlrabi, slice very thinly on a mandolin (be careful as it is very sharp) – or use a very sharp knife – and put the slices into a bowl. Heat the cream and milk in a small pan together with the crushed garlic, butter and nutmeg.

Pour the warm cream mixture over the kohlrabi and season. Make sure all the pieces of kohlrabi have a light covering of cream.

Carefully layer the kohlrabi, piece by piece, into a baking dish that will take all the slices so it is full. Pack the slices down quite tightly and securely. Bake for 45 minutes, until the kohlrabi is tender. Serve.

watermelon and feta salad

I love the contrasting, fresh sweetness of the melon with the salty tang of the feta in this salad. It's great by itself, or served with grilled sea bass, chargrilled lamb, or some barbecued prawns – perfect for an outdoor summer meal.

SERVES 6

½ watermelon (use the rest in a fruit salad or
    for a breakfast platter)
50g/2oz pine nuts
225g/8oz feta cheese
1 tbsp shredded mint
splash of olive oil

Cut the watermelon in half again, scoop out the seeds and peel the skin with a sharp knife. Cut the melon into wedges and arrange them on a serving platter.

Toast the pine nuts in a dry frying pan, shaking the pan often so they don't burn. Sprinkle them over the watermelon. Crumble the feta over the top and scatter with the mint. Drizzle with olive oil and serve.

savoy cabbage, chestnut and gruyère bake

This is surprisingly tasty. One client of mine once ate four portions of it with roast chicken at one sitting! It goes well with any traditionally English fare – a Sunday roast or warming winter casserole would be perfect.

SERVES 4–6

1 Savoy cabbage

1 onion

1 garlic clove

2 bacon rashers (optional)

50g/2oz butter

225g/8oz peeled whole vacuum-packed chestnuts

3 tbsp white wine

salt and freshly ground black pepper

2 tbsp double cream

150g/5oz mature Gruyère cheese

Quarter the cabbage and cut out and discard the central core. Carefully slice the cabbage thinly and set aside. Finely slice the onion and chop the garlic and bacon, if using.

Melt the butter in a large saucepan and gently fry the onion and bacon until pale golden, then add the garlic and fry for another minute. Add the cabbage, the chestnuts, breaking them in with your fingers, and the white wine. Season, cover with a lid and simmer for about 5 minutes, stirring if necessary, until the cabbage is starting to soften. Remove the lid, pour in the cream and continue cooking, covered, until the cabbage is just cooked, about 5–8 more minutes. Pour the mixture into a gratin dish.

Grate the Gruyère cheese over the top and brown under a hot grill for 5–10 minutes until golden and bubbly.

proper greek salad

The Greek in me comes out again... A Greek salad can be wonderful and it's very basic, but many people add unnecessary ingredients and spoil the flavour. It's important to use a good olive oil. The Greeks have some of the lowest rates of heart disease in the world, and consume the most olive oil – a miracle ingredient if ever there was one.

SERVES 4

1 cucumber
4 beef tomatoes
1 red onion
225g/8oz feta cheese
125g/4oz black kalamata olives
1 tsp dried oregano
extra-virgin Greek olive oil, for drizzling

Peel the cucumber, then cut it in half lengthways and chop it into large pieces. Put the cucumber in a serving bowl. Cut the tomatoes into rough, large pieces, discarding the top pieces of core, and add to the bowl. Peel the onion and cut into thick slices and toss with the cucumber and tomatoes.

Crumble the feta over the top and toss on the olives. Sprinkle the oregano on the feta and douse all liberally with olive oil. Lovely!

roasted cherry tomatoes and baby onions

For times when you want some no-nonsense food! This is a dream served with a nice, fat, juicy, garlicky steak.

SERVES 4

225g/8oz small shallots
splash of olive oil
400g/13oz cherry tomatoes (you can use a
    mixture of red and yellow if you like)
splash of balsamic vinegar
½ bunch of basil, shredded
salt and freshly ground black pepper

Preheat the oven to 200°C/400°F/gas 6. Peel the shallots, then place them in a small roasting tin and toss with a splash of olive oil. Roast them for 15–20 minutes until starting to turn golden.

Add the tomatoes and balsamic vinegar and roast for another 15 minutes, or until the tomatoes are beginning to soften, but still keep their shape. Remove from the oven, stir in the basil, season and serve.

pernod–braised fennel

I've got a thing about aniseed flavours. The flavour of the fennel is intensified by the Pernod and is gorgeous with fish, especially sea bass.

SERVES 4–6
3 fennel bulbs
splash of olive oil
100ml/3½fl oz Pernod
1 litre/1¾ pints vegetable stock
salt and freshly ground black pepper

Cut each fennel bulb into about 6 wedges. Heat the oil in a large, deep frying pan, add the fennel and brown on each side. Pour in the Pernod and let it cook for 5 minutes, uncovered.

Add the stock, cover with a sheet of greaseproof paper and continue cooking gently for 20 minutes or until tender. Season if necessary, lift the fennel out with a slotted spoon and serve.

ginger-glazed roasted beetroot

I love beetroot because it's pink and somehow the fuschia juices always seem to get on everything! What fun!

SERVES 4
4 raw beetroots
2.5cm/1in piece of fresh root ginger
olive oil, for drizzling
salt and freshly ground black pepper
1 tsp runny honey

Preheat the oven to 180°C/350°F/gas 4. Peel and quarter the beetroots. Cut the ginger into small strips.

Mix the beetroots and ginger in a small roasting tin or on a baking sheet, and mix with a generous drizzle of olive oil and some seasoning. Drizzle with the honey and roast for 40 minutes, or until done. Serve.

spiced red cabbage

This is a lovely, warming dish. It works really well with the Venison with pink peppercorn crust (see page 93) or the roast chicken (see page 84), and reminds me of Christmas.

SERVES 4

1 onion
3 streaky bacon rashers
½ red cabbage
splash of olive oil
2 cooking apples
5 whole cloves
½ tsp ground mixed spice
¼–½ tsp freshly grated nutmeg
100ml/3½fl oz red wine
3–4 tbsp port
2 tbsp red wine vinegar
1 tbsp light muscovado sugar
salt and freshly ground black pepper

Chop the onion and bacon into small pieces. Finely slice the cabbage. Heat a generous splash of olive oil in a large saucepan and gently fry the onion and bacon (some fat will come out of the bacon), then stir in the cabbage and fry all of it, covered, for a few minutes.

Peel, core and dice the apples. Stir them into the cabbage with the spices, wine, port, vinegar and sugar. Season well. Lower the heat and simmer for 30–40 minutes until the cabbage is softened, stirring occasionally. Serve when cooked and glossy.

cauliflower mash

This is a great replacement for regular mash when you want time off from potatoes.

SERVES 4
1 head of cauliflower
500ml/17fl oz milk
splash of double cream
25g/1oz butter
pinch of freshly grated nutmeg
salt and freshly ground black pepper

Break the cauliflower into small florets. Pour the milk and 500ml/17fl oz water into a large saucepan. Add the cauliflower, bring to the boil and simmer, covered, until tender, about 15 minutes.

Drain the cauliflower well, then tip back into the pan and add the cream, butter and nutmeg. Blitz with a hand-blender until fine (or use a potato masher), season and serve.

white bean and roast garlic mash

When garlic is roasted whole like this, it's fantastic. It takes on a lovely, sweet, subtle flavour and you can use it as a spread on crostini, mixed with cheese, or with anything... Here I've mixed it with butter beans, which makes a great accompaniment for lamb.

SERVES 4
1 whole garlic bulb
2 x 400g/13oz cans butter beans, drained and rinsed
3 tbsp vegetable stock or water
1 tbsp chopped sage
1 tbsp chopped rosemary
100ml/3½fl oz olive oil
salt and freshly ground black pepper

Preheat the oven to 180°C/350°F/gas 4. Wrap the garlic in foil and roast for about 20 minutes, or until really soft.

Meanwhile, heat the beans in a saucepan with the stock or water and the herbs. Add the oil and garlic – just squeeze the base of the bulb and the inside of each clove will pop out with a bit of encouragement: gorgeous! Continue cooking for 5 minutes to combine. Season well, then roughly mash with a potato masher and serve.

nutty puy lentil and goat's cheese salad

The tang of the goat's cheese goes beautifully with the nuttiness of the lentils in this salad. Great on its own, it's also a good side dish for grilled or barbecued chicken or lamb.

SERVES 4

50g/2oz walnuts
50g/2oz hazelnuts
250g/8½oz Puy lentils
1 red onion, finely chopped
small bunch of flat-leaf parsley, chopped
225g/8oz goat's cheese, crumbled

FOR THE DRESSING
4 tbsp extra-virgin olive oil
2 tbsp balsamic vinegar
salt and freshly ground black pepper

Heat a dry frying pan, add the nuts, then lightly fry until just turning golden. Tip the nuts on to a board and chop them roughly. Set aside. Mix all the dressing ingredients together and set aside.

Put the lentils in a medium saucepan and cover with water. Do not salt the water as this hardens the lentils. Simmer, covered, for about 30–40 minutes, or until just cooked and still keeping their shape. Drain well, tip back into the pan and stir in the chopped onion, parsley and the dressing. Season to taste. Pile on to a serving dish and serve topped with the crumbled goat's cheese and a sprinkling of the nuts.

thai papaya salad

This dish is all about balancing the sweetness of the papaya with the salty shrimps and sour lime. It is a delicious side dish for any of the Thai-inspired recipes such as the Curried buckwheat noodles (see page 115).

SERVES 4

1 shallot, finely chopped
25g/1oz dried shrimp, roughly crushed
½ garlic clove, finely chopped
1 red chilli, deseeded and finely chopped
1 tbsp Thai fish sauce
juice of 2 limes
2 semi-ripe papayas, or green ones if you can get them
1 tbsp shredded coriander
50g/2oz chopped roasted or raw peanuts

Mix together the shallot, dried shrimp, garlic, chilli, fish sauce and lime juice to taste.

Halve the papayas, scoop out the seeds and peel off the skin. Cut the papayas into very thin slices, then transfer to a bowl or lay on a serving platter. Pour on the dressing, scatter over the coriander and peanuts and serve.

stir-fried broccoli with chilli and garlic

Broccoli is packed with a feast of vitamins and antioxidants – you really can't eat enough of it! Chilli and garlic are also great immune-boosting ingredients, so this is truly good health on a plate. This is great with pretty much all the dishes.

SERVES 4

1 large or 2 small heads of broccoli
splash of olive oil
2 garlic cloves, thinly sliced
pinch of dried chilli flakes
salt and freshly ground black pepper

Bring a large saucepan of water to the boil. Cut the broccoli into florets and drop them into the boiling water. Simmer until just done, but still with some crunch, then drain in a colander and refresh under running cold water. Set aside.

Heat the olive oil in a wok or deep frying pan. Add the garlic and chilli and fry briefly until the garlic is golden, but don't overcook or the garlic will taste bitter. Immediately tip in the broccoli and heat through. Season well and serve.

vietnamese radish, carrot and mint salad

This salad is like a detox on a plate, it's so clean and fresh-tasting! Because it's so virtuous, I'd be inclined to serve it with some shredded, poached chicken, but it works well with any Asian dishes.

SERVES 4

3 large carrots
1 white radish (mooli)
100ml/3½fl oz white rice vinegar
½ tsp Thai fish sauce
small bunch of mint
1 red chilli, deseeded
75g/3oz roasted or raw peanuts

Peel the carrots and radish and cut into thin julienne strips. Put on a platter and pour over the rice vinegar and fish sauce. Toss together. Shred the mint and slice the red chilli.

To serve, scatter the mint, chilli and peanuts over the top of the radish and carrot salad.

roasted ratatouille

This is different from traditional ratatouille, because it's cooked by roasting the vegetables rather than as a stew on top of the stove. You can practically smell Provence while you make it.

SERVES 4
1 aubergine
1 red pepper, deseeded
1 yellow pepper, deseeded
2 courgettes
2 red onions
3 plum tomatoes
3 garlic cloves
1 thyme sprig
2 bay leaves
1 tsp dried *herbes de provence*
generous splash of olive oil
salt and freshly ground black pepper
handful of shredded basil, to serve

Preheat the oven to 200°C/400°F/gas 6. Cut the aubergine and peppers into large chunks. Cut the courgettes into thickish slices and the onions into wedges. Quarter the tomatoes.

Spread all the vegetables in a single layer on a large baking sheet. Crush the garlic over the top, scatter with the thyme and bay leaves, then add a sprinkling of the Provençale herbs and a generous splash of olive oil. Gently toss everything together, spread out again in a single layer, season well and roast for about 30 minutes, or until the vegetables are starting to turn golden around the edges, shaking the baking sheet half-way through. Serve scattered with the basil.

roast squash
with amaretti crust

The idea of mixing squash with almond may
seem strange, but it's traditionally Italian.
Travelling through Italy, we stopped near
Lake Garda and had some amazing amaretti and
pumpkin ravioli, served with sage butter.
Gorgeous! This is my adaptation. It goes well
with Veal escalopes with porcini (see page 97),
or as a potato replacement.

SERVES 3–4
1 butternut squash
splash of olive oil
salt and freshly ground black pepper
splash of amaretto liqueur
3 amaretti biscuits, crushed
1 tbsp roughly chopped flat-leaf parsley

Preheat the oven to 200°C/400°F/gas 6. Cut the
squash into quarters, then scoop out the seeds
and cut off the skin with a sharp knife. Cut the
squash into thick wedges and put in a small
roasting tin, or on a baking sheet. Rub in the
olive oil, season with salt and pepper and roast
for 30 minutes, or until beginning to turn golden
around the edges.

Pour over a splash of amaretto and scatter over
the crushed amaretti biscuits. Continue to roast
for 10 minutes. Sprinkle the squash with the
parsley and serve.

little gem and rocket salad
with mustard and parmesan creamy dressing

The creamy rich taste of this dressing turns
a simple green salad into something far more
decadent. It's the perfect partner for any grilled
or roasted meat.

SERVES 4

2 heads of Little Gem lettuce
75–100g/3–3½oz rocket
50g/2oz Parmesan shavings

FOR THE DRESSING

2 egg yolks
1 tsp Dijon mustard
½ tsp wholegrain (Meaux) mustard
1 tsp Splenda sweetener
300ml/½ pint vegetable oil
2 tbsp white wine vinegar
50g/2oz Parmesan cheese, grated
salt and freshly ground black pepper

Make the dressing. Put the egg yolks, mustards
and sweetener in a mixing bowl and whisk
together. Pour in the oil very gradually at first,
whisking all the time. It should start to thicken
after about half the oil has been added, then you
can pour it in more quickly. When all the oil
has been added, whisk in the wine vinegar and
about 2 tablespoons water, to create a thick,
smooth dressing. Stir in the grated Parmesan
and check the seasoning.

Break the Little Gem lettuces into separate leaves
and mix with the rocket in a bowl. Dress the
salad with enough of the dressing to coat but not
drench the leaves. (Keep any leftover dressing in
the fridge for 3–4 days.) Serve sprinkled with the
Parmesan shavings.

warm pea, broad bean and asparagus fricassée

This recipe uses frozen peas and beans as they're often sweeter and more tender than when fresh. This sounds strange, but unless you can buy them fresh from a quality retailer and at the peak of their season, they often disappoint and taste woody and flavourless. I love serving this side dish with caramelised scallops wrapped in Parma ham, roast salmon or grilled trout, but it's also a lovely accompaniment to roast or grilled meat.

SERVES 4
250g/8½ oz frozen broad beans, thawed
250g/8½ oz frozen petits pois, thawed
1 bunch of asparagus
1 bunch of chives
50g/2oz butter
salt and freshly ground black pepper

Deskin the broad beans. Do this by tearing the skin at one end and popping out the lovely little green inside. Mix the peas and beans together.

Bring a saucepan of water to the boil. Trim the woody ends from the asparagus and cook in the water for 4 minutes, or until tender-crisp. Drain in a colander and refresh under cold water.

Chop the chives. In a deep frying pan, melt the butter, then add the beans, peas and asparagus. Season and heat through. Stir in the chives and serve.

lentil dahl

A staple dish in India, this quick and satisfying lentil recipe is healthy comfort food. It's lovely and warming when the weather is cold.

SERVES 4

1 onion

2 garlic cloves

1 tbsp vegetable oil

300g/10oz red lentils

75g/3oz ready-to-eat dried apricots, chopped

small handful of chopped fresh coriander

juice of 1 lemon

FOR THE SPICE MIX

½ tsp ground cinnamon

½ tsp ground cumin

½ tsp ground coriander

½ tsp curry powder

¼ tsp ground turmeric

¼ tsp chilli powder

Mix all the spices together for the spice mix. Chop the onion and garlic. Heat the oil in a medium saucepan. Add the onion and fry with the garlic and spices until the onion starts to soften. Tip in the lentils and apricots, then pour in enough water to cover the lentils by about 5cm/2in. Bring to the boil, lower the heat and simmer, covered, for 30–40 minutes, or until the lentils are cooked.

To serve, stir in the fresh coriander and season to taste with salt, pepper and lemon juice.

artichokes à la grecque

Artichokes are fantastically good for you – they are reported to lower blood cholesterol and are also a diuretic. One constituent of artichoke – cynarin – has even been formulated as a drug to lower cholesterol, and is known as a 'liver protective' too. This method of cooking in the sauce also works well for baby vegetables (see page 39), and even mushrooms (just trim them and simmer for 5 minutes). As well as making a superb side dish, the artichokes are a great addition to an antipasto plate.

SERVES 4
250ml/8fl oz white wine
juice of 1 lemon (reserve the lemon halves)
1 plum tomato, chopped
1 tsp coriander seeds
1 garlic clove
2 shallots, sliced
1 tsp black peppercorns
1 tsp dried oregano
3 tbsp olive oil
salt and freshly ground black pepper
4 globe artichokes
1 tbsp chopped parsley

Put all the ingredients into a saucepan, except for the artichokes and parsley, and pour in about 750ml//1¼ pints water. Bring to the boil, then lower the heat and simmer for 10 minutes.

Meanwhile prepare the artichokes. Break or cut off the stem at the base of each one. Carefully pluck off and discard the tough leaves, one by one, until you reach the greener and more delicate leaves. Rub the artichokes all over with the reserved lemon halves, to prevent them discolouring. With a small, sharp knife, carefully trim the bases, so that each one is neat and smooth, and trim off the top of the leaves.

Place the artichokes in the liquid and simmer for 30 minutes. Lift the artichokes out of the pan with a slotted spoon and set aside. Bring the cooking liquid to the boil, and cook until reduced by half, about 20 minutes.

When the artichokes are cool enough to handle, remove the remaining outside leaves, so that you are left with the base (heart). With a teaspoon, scoop out the choke (the hairy bit in the middle). Trim the edges and cut each artichoke into quarters.

Put the artichoke hearts back into the reduced sauce with the parsley, allow to cool, then chill until ready to serve. It will keep in the fridge for up to 2–3 days.

decadent desserts

Proceed with caution: these desserts may damage your health! Yes, I know, after my lecture on the evils of sugar and refined carbs, I've gone mad and included a whole chapter of them. Well, ideally I don't want you to eat any desserts, but let's get real – sometimes you just want something sweet.

Still, rather than buying chemical-ridden, 'low-fat', plastic desserts, I recommend you make your own. Not only is this more satisfying, but you'll see just how much sugar goes into a normal pudding. These desserts should satisfy your cravings enough so that you don't over-indulge. A home-made dessert that uses the best ingredients is far better for you than a shop-bought version. Just don't tuck in *too* often!

irish coffee profiteroles

Everyone loves profiteroles and these, made with a coffee-cream filling, are to die for.

MAKES ABOUT 20

FOR THE CRÈME PATISSIÈRE
1 vanilla pod
250ml/8fl oz milk
25g/1oz cornflour
75g/3oz caster sugar
4 egg yolks
3 tbsp strong black coffee
2 tbsp double cream
1 shot of whisky

FOR THE CHOUX PASTRY
75g/3oz butter
pinch of salt
125g/4oz plain flour
3 eggs, beaten

FOR THE COFFEE ICING
200g/7oz icing sugar
about 1½–2 tbsp strong black coffee

Make the crème patissière first. Split the vanilla pod in half lengthways and scrape the seeds into a medium saucepan, then add the milk and drop in the vanilla pod. Heat gently. While the milk is heating, beat the cornflour, sugar and egg yolks together in a heatproof bowl, just enough to mix them.

When the milk has just come to the boil, remove the vanilla pod and pour the milk into the egg mixture, whisking all the time. Pour the mixture back into the saucepan and gently reheat again, stirring all the time to make sure it doesn't burn.

Cook over a low heat for about 4–6 minutes or until the mixture is thick enough to coat the back of a wooden spoon. Take the pan off the heat and stir in the coffee. Leave to cool, and, to stop a skin from forming, cover with clingfilm, pressing it right down on to the surface of the crème. Allow to cool, then chill.

Now make the choux pastry. Line a baking sheet with silicone paper or parchment paper. Preheat the oven to 200°C/400°F/gas 6. Pour 175ml/6fl oz water into a saucepan, add the butter and salt and bring to the boil. When it is boiling really rapidly, add the flour all in one go, take off the heat immediately and beat quickly with a wooden spoon. The mixture should come away from the sides of the pan the more you beat. Cool the pastry slightly, then gradually add enough of the beaten eggs, beating well between each addition, until the mixture reaches a dropping consistency.

Using a teaspoon, drop balls of the mix (about cherry-tomato size) in lines on the prepared baking sheet. Bake for 30–35 minutes until puffed, golden and crispy. If you take them out too soon, they will deflate. Remove and leave to cool on a wire rack. Beat the double cream with a fork to thicken, then fold into the crème patissière with the whisky. Make a small slit in the middle of each bun with a sharp knife, then pipe or spoon the crème into the choux buns.

For the icing, just mix the icing sugar and enough coffee together to make a thickish, smooth icing and dunk the buns in to give a good layer on top. Serve. (Once filled, they should be eaten within a few hours, or the pastry will become too soft.)

coconut tart with lime glaze

This is a set custard tart – an Anglicised version of the little coconut custards they make in Indonesia. Lime and coconut are a fantastic combination, as the lime glaze cuts through the richness of the coconut beautifully. I often make a tropical fruit salad to serve alongside, or just serve the tart with some passionfruit quarters.

SERVES 6–8
300g/10oz butter
175g/6oz icing sugar
1 vanilla pod
pinch of salt
125g/4oz eggs, beaten (about 2 eggs)
75g/3oz ground almonds
500g/1lb strong plain flour

FOR THE COCONUT CUSTARD
250ml/8fl oz double cream
250ml/8fl oz coconut cream
4 egg yolks
125g/4oz caster sugar
1 shot of Malibu

FOR THE LIME GLAZE
grated zest and juice of 2 limes
150g/5oz caster sugar

First, make the pastry – this is best done in an electric mixer. Split the vanilla pod lengthways and scrape the seeds into the bowl. Add the butter, sugar and salt and cream together until just mixed: do not overwork. Gradually add the beaten eggs, then the ground almonds. Finally mix in the flour – again, do not overwork the dough. Shape the dough into a ball, wrap in clingfilm and chill for 1 hour before using.

Preheat the oven to 180°C/350°F/gas 4. Roll the pastry out and use to line a 20cm/8in fluted flan tin, about 3cm/1¼in deep. Place the tin on a baking sheet. Line the pastry case with grease-proof paper, fill with baking beans and bake 'blind' for 10–12 minutes, or until the pastry is set. Carefully lift out the paper and beans and return the pastry case to the oven for a further 5 minutes, or until the pastry is cooked but not too coloured.

Lower the oven temperature to 160°C/325°F/ gas 3. Make the custard. Gently heat the two creams together. Mix the egg yolks and sugar together. When the cream mixture is just boiling, slowly pour it on to the egg mix, whisking all the time. Stir in the Malibu. Pour the custard into the (preferably warm) pastry case and bake for 30 minutes or until set, being careful not to overcook. Leave to cool.

Now make the lime glaze. Put the lime juice and sugar into a small saucepan. Make sure all the sugar is moistened, and add a couple of tablespoons water if necessary. Heat the mixture over a gentle heat, stirring to dissolve the sugar. When the sugar is dissolved, bring the mixture to the boil and simmer for about 2 minutes, until it has formed a thick syrup. Remove from the heat and stir in the lime zest. Carefully pour the glaze over the tart and spread evenly.

lavender crème brûlées with langues de chat

I love using flowers in my cooking. It used to be common practice in English recipes years ago, and I think the idea should be resurrected. It's one way of introducing a bit of femininity to a tough old world.

SERVES 4

FOR THE CRÈME BRÛLÉES
600ml/1 pint double cream
1 vanilla pod
1 tsp lavender flowers
8 egg yolks
50g/2oz caster sugar, plus extra for
    caramelising

FOR THE LANGUES DE CHAT BISCUITS
125g/4oz butter, at room temperature
125g/4oz caster sugar
3 large egg whites
125g/4oz plain flour
2 tsp lavender flowers and/or dried rose
    petals, crushed

Make the crème brûlées. Pour the cream into a saucepan. Split the vanilla pod lengthways, scrape the seeds into the cream and drop in the pod and the lavender flowers. Bring slowly to the boil, then take off the heat, set aside and allow to rest for 20 minutes. Preheat the oven to 160°C/325°F/gas 3. Mix the egg yolks and sugar together. Reheat the cream, then whisk it into the egg mix. Strain the mixture into a jug.

Sit 4 (about 175ml/6fl oz) ramekin dishes into a large roasting tin, then divide the brûlée mix between them. Pour enough boiling water into the tin to come half-way up the sides of the ramekins, and bake for 30 minutes, or until just set but slightly wobbly in the centre. Do not overcook. Carefully lift the ramekins out of the water and set aside to cool.

Now make the biscuits. Turn the oven up to 200°C/400°F/gas 6. Line a baking sheet with silicone paper or baking parchment. Beat the butter slightly, then beat in the sugar until light and fluffy. Whisk the egg whites until stiff, then fold them gradually into the butter mixture. Sift the flour and fold it into the mixture.

Fit a large piping bag with a medium plain nozzle and spoon in the mixture. Pipe it in 7.5cm/3in-long fingers (about the thickness of a pen) on to the baking sheet, allowing a little space between them. Sprinkle with the flowers or petals, then bake for 5–7 minutes until pale golden around the edges.

Sprinkle the tops of the brûlées with extra caster sugar, about 1 tablespoon per ramekin, and caramelise each one with a blow-torch (or place them under a hot grill) until dark brown. Serve with the biscuits.

strawberry shortbreads

You can't beat some of the old-fashioned flavour combinations. Strawberries, cream and shortbread – brilliant! The shortbread recipe makes a substantial amount, but the dough keeps so well in the freezer, I prefer to make a large batch and freeze half if I'm feeding fewer people. What better excuse to have freshly baked shortbread twice! The quantities for the strawberry cream are easily scaled down.

SERVES 12

FOR THE SHORTBREAD

300g/10oz plain flour
150g/5oz caster sugar, plus extra for
    sprinkling
250g/8½oz butter
1 vanilla pod

FOR THE STRAWBERRY CREAM

250g/8½oz strawberries, hulled, plus extra
    whole ones to decorate
150ml/¼ pint double cream
1 tbsp icing sugar

First make the shortbread. It's easiest to do this in an electric mixer if you have one. Mix the flour and sugar together. Then cube the butter and add to the mixture. Cut the vanilla pod in half and scrape the seeds into the bowl. Using the dough hook, mix until well combined (with no lumps of butter left) and the dough starts to hold together. Do not over-mix.

Cut the ball in half. Roll out each piece between 2 pieces of silicone or parchment paper, to a thickness of about 5mm/¼in. Place the pieces of dough on baking sheets or a board and chill in the fridge for about 30 minutes. (If you are halving the recipe, wrap 1 piece in clingfilm and store it in the freezer. It will keep for 2–3 months and can be cut and baked from frozen.)

Preheat the oven to 150°C/300°F/gas 2. Using a 6cm/2½in round cutter, cut the shortbread into 12 circles. Lay them on a baking sheet and bake for about 20 minutes. Do not let them colour; just allow them to turn a pale biscuit colour. Sprinkle with caster sugar while still warm, then leave to cool completely on a wire rack.

Chop the hulled strawberries into small pieces. Whip the double cream and icing sugar together to form soft peaks and fold in the strawberries. For each serving, sandwich 2 biscuits together with a big dollop of the strawberry cream. Serve decorated with whole strawberries.

almond panna cottas with loganberry compote

I love using amaretto instead of the more usual rum to make this set Italian cream. I've used loganberries for the compote because they keep their shape so well, but you can use raspberries if you prefer.

SERVES 6

FOR THE PANNA COTTAS
6 sheets of leaf gelatine
2 vanilla pods, split lengthways
400ml/14fl oz double cream
250ml/8fl oz milk
225g/8oz caster sugar
1 shot of amaretto liqueur

FOR THE COMPOTE
75g/3oz caster sugar
225g/8oz loganberries

Make the panna cottas. Put the gelatine into a bowl, cover with cold water and set aside. Scrape the seeds from the vanilla pods into a saucepan. Add the cream, milk and sugar and heat through. Lift the gelatine out of the water and squeeze out any excess liquid. As the cream and milk come up to the boil, take the pan off the heat and stir in the softened gelatine, stirring until it is completely dissolved. Then pour the mixture through a sieve into a bowl and add the amaretto.

You can pour directly into the moulds now, but all the vanilla seeds will sink to the bottom (so they will be on the top when turned out). To stop this from happening, put the big bowl into the fridge and chill. Whisk every 30 minutes or so to distribute the vanilla seeds evenly.

When the mixture is starting to jellify, but not set, divide it evenly between 6 x 150ml/¼ pint small metal pudding moulds and put in the fridge to set completely (about 2 hours).

Meanwhile, make the compote. Heat the sugar with 2 tablespoons water over a low heat, stirring to dissolve. Add the berries and cook for 1–2 minutes, until just softened but still keeping their shape. Remove from the heat and leave to cool. Unmould the panna cottas and serve with the compote.

turkish delight pavlova

This looks very pretty and is a great dessert for Christmastime. As extra decoration, you can drizzle on some melted chocolate or, for a completely magical effect, sprinkle with edible gold dust if you can find it.

SERVES 6–8

FOR THE PAVLOVA BASE
4 egg whites
pinch of salt
225g/8oz caster sugar
1 tsp cornflour
1 tsp lemon juice

FOR THE TOPPING
400ml/14fl oz double cream
50g/2oz icing sugar, sifted
1 tbsp rosewater
175–225g/6–8oz rose Turkish delight

Make the pavlova base. Preheat the oven to 140°C/275°F/gas 1. Line a baking sheet with silicone or parchment paper. Using an electric mixer, whisk the egg whites until they form soft peaks. Add the salt and continue whisking until stiff. Gradually add the sugar a spoonful at a time, continuing to whisk until the mixture is thick and glossy. Whisk in the cornflour and lemon juice.

Spoon the meringue on to the prepared baking sheet in a 25cm/10in circle with a slight dent in the middle. Bake for 1 hour. The outside should be pale golden brown and the inside should be marshmallowy. When it is cooked, remove the pavlova from the oven, peel off the lining paper and leave to cool.

To make the topping, whip the cream to soft peaks, then fold in the icing sugar and rosewater. Spoon and spread the cream on to the pavlova. Cut the Turkish delight into smaller cubes and use as decoration.

summer fruit crumble

Crumble is a great, quick dessert to pull out of the bag. It's always really well received and has the back-to-basics, comfort-food factor.

SERVES 6–8
FOR THE TOPPING
250g/8½oz plain flour
250g/8½oz butter, cut in pieces
125g/4oz caster sugar
1 tbsp demerara sugar
50g/2oz ground or flaked almonds

FOR THE FILLING
450g/14½oz frozen mixed summer fruits, thawed, or fresh seasonal summer fruits
50g/2oz caster sugar
ice cream or custard, to serve

Preheat the oven to 180°C/350°F/gas 4. First make the crumble topping. Rub the flour, butter and caster sugar together, lifting the mixture as you go, to get more air in. Rub until the mixture has the consistency of rough breadcrumbs.

For the filling. put the summer fruits and caster sugar into a saucepan and bring just to the boil. Simmer for 2 minutes, or until the fruits have softened, then take off the heat. Pour the fruits into a deep baking dish. Cover with the crumble mixture, sprinkle on the demerara sugar and the almonds and bake for 30–40 minutes until golden on top. Serve with ice cream or custard.

great-grandma's lemon pudding with blueberry clotted cream

My great-grandma was a professional cook in the 1920s and 1930s, and reputedly cooked for the Queen Mother in a freezing-cold hunting lodge in Scotland. Even in her seventies, she was cooking dinner parties for the local 'gentry' in Cheshire, so she must have been doing something right! This pudding is one of her recipes, handed down to my mother. I call it the 'magic' lemon sponge as it separates into a light lemon sponge with a lemon curd mix underneath.

SERVES 4
225g/8oz caster sugar
1 tbsp butter, softened
2 eggs, separated
finely grated zest and juice of 1 lemon
2 tbsp plain flour
300ml/½ pint milk
225g/8oz clotted cream
150g/5oz blueberries

Preheat the oven to 150°C/300°F/gas 2. Beat the sugar, butter, egg yolks, lemon zest and juice all together. Stir in the flour, mix well, then beat in the milk to make a soft, smooth mixture.

In a separate, non-greasy bowl, whisk the egg whites until stiff, then carefully fold them into the lemon sponge mixture. Pour the mixture into a buttered ovenproof dish. Place the dish in a roasting tin and pour hot water into the tin until it is just below the top of the dish. This stops the pudding from cooking too quickly and keeps it moist. Bake for about 45 minutes, until the top is pale golden and feels bouncy like a sponge.

Meanwhile, stir the clotted cream to soften it. Using a fork, lightly crush the blueberries and stir them into the cream.

When ready to serve, scoop out a lovely, large portion of pud and top with a generous dollop of blueberry clotted cream – good, old-fashioned pudding bliss.

raspberry possets with pistachio biscotti

The traditional recipe for possets uses lemon, but when I was experimenting one day I made this raspberry version. These desserts are really yummy and a very glamorous pink colour.

SERVES 6

FOR THE POSSETS

400ml/14fl oz raspberry purée, bought or home-made
900ml/1½ pints double cream
250g/8oz caster sugar
juice of 1 lemon

FOR THE BISCOTTI

225g/8oz pistachios, left whole
250g/8½oz plain flour
150g/5oz caster sugar
1 tsp baking powder
3 eggs

For the possets, sieve the raspberry purée to remove any seeds if this hasn't already been done. Put the double cream and sugar into a saucepan and bring to the boil. Remove from the heat and stir in the raspberry purée and lemon juice. Leave to cool slightly.

When the mixture is cool, carefully pour it into 6 wine glasses and chill until set, which should take about 2 hours.

Then make the biscotti. Preheat the oven to 180°C/350°F/gas 4. Tip all the ingredients, except the eggs, into an electric mixer and mix together. Add the eggs and blend to form a stiff dough. Remove the dough and shape it into 2 large, flat logs, about 30cm/12in long, 12cm/5in wide and 2.5cm/1in high. Lay them on a large baking sheet and bake for about 20 minutes or until the logs are cooked throughout but not too brown. When they are cool enough to handle, lift the logs on to a board and slice very thinly (about 5mm/¼in thick) on an extreme diagonal, then place the separate biscuits on 1 or 2 baking sheets. Bake for another 10 minutes, or until pale golden brown and crisp. (You should make about 25–30 biscotti, but any left over will keep in an airtight tin for about a week and are great with coffee.) Serve the possets with the biscuits.

cinnamon custard tart with cider brandy–soaked sultanas

I'm turning into a real Somerset girl in my old age! I spent a lot of my childhood and teenage years in the West Country and never thought much of it (you don't think much of anything when you're a teenager!). Now I really appreciate all the amazing produce that is made down there. Whenever I get a chance, I go to Burrow Hill cider farm and stock up on cider and other goodies. I especially love their 15-year-old cider brandy. It certainly compares well to French calvados and is fantastically aromatic. I use it in this recipe to soak my sultanas, but any calvados or cider brandy will do.

SERVES 8–10
75g/3oz sultanas
100ml/3½fl oz Somerset cider brandy
1 quantity sweet pastry (see page 151)

FOR THE CUSTARD
750ml/1¼ pints double cream
125g/4oz caster sugar
11 egg yolks
1 tsp ground cinnamon
sprinkling of freshly grated nutmeg

The night before you start making this dish, soak the sultanas in the cider brandy.

Make the sweet pastry, wrap and chill. While it is chilling, make the custard. Pour the cream into a saucepan, then place over a very low heat. Don't let the cream come to the boil. Beat the sugar and egg yolks together with the cinnamon in a large mixing bowl just to combine. Do not over-whisk: you don't want any bubbles. (The egg whites can be frozen in batches (remember to label) and used for meringue desserts, such as Turkish delight pavlova (see page 156), or Low-fat hazelnut cake (see page 168).) Carefully add the hot cream to the egg mixture, stirring as you do so, until mixed into a custard. Set aside.

Preheat the oven to 190°C/375°F/gas 5. Roll out the pastry and use to line a deep 23cm/9in round flan tin. Place the tin on a baking sheet. Line the pastry case with greaseproof paper, fill with baking beans and bake 'blind' for 12–15 minutes, or until the pastry is set. Carefully lift out the paper and beans and return the pastry case to the oven for a further 5 minutes, or until the pastry is cooked but not too coloured. Lower the oven temperature to 140°C/275°F/gas 1.

Drain the sultanas of any cider brandy that is left. Spread the sultanas in a thin layer on the base of the tart case and pour the custard through a sieve over the top. Sprinkle with a little grated nutmeg. Bake for 40 minutes, or until the custard is just set but still wobbly. Cool and serve at room temperature.

strawberry salad with pink peppercorn ice-cream

Surprisingly, peppercorns and strawberries are a traditional combination, used in many old English recipes; it's only relatively recently that pepper has been limited to savoury dishes. This recipe does need an ice-cream machine. I haven't explained how to make the ice-cream by hand because, as Shirley Conran once said, 'Life is too short to stuff a mushroom'. I don't mind stuffing mushrooms, but won't stretch to hand-churning ice cream!

SERVES 6
400g/13oz strawberries

FOR THE ICE CREAM
7 egg yolks
50g/2oz caster sugar
1 vanilla pod, split lengthways
500ml/17fl oz double cream
500ml/17fl oz milk
1 tsp cracked pink peppercorns, plus extra to serve

Make the ice cream. Mix the egg yolks and sugar together in a largish bowl. Scrape the seeds from the vanilla pod into a saucepan, add the pod, the cream, milk and crushed peppercorns and heat slowly. When the mixture is just coming to the boil, take it off the heat and pour it slowly into the egg mixture, whisking all the time. You must whisk while you add the hot cream mix, or it will cook the egg. Pour back into the pan and very gently heat through. Do not boil as it will curdle, just thicken slightly, then take off the heat and leave to cool.

Follow the instructions on your ice-cream machine for churning and freezing the cooled custard. When the ice cream is ready, spoon into a freezer container and put in the freezer.

To make the strawberry salad, hull and halve the strawberries, then serve with scoops of ice cream and a sprinkling of cracked peppercorns.

rosewater cheesecakes with sweet pistachio pesto

These little cakes are very cute. The flavours of pistachio and rosewater echo Middle Eastern recipes, although medieval English dishes also made use of the delicate taste of flowers.

SERVES 6

125g/4oz digestive biscuits
50g/2oz butter, melted
225g/8oz full-fat cream cheese, at room temperature
50g/2oz caster sugar
3 tbsp soured cream
1 egg, plus 1 egg yolk
½ tsp rosewater
1 tsp lemon juice
1 tbsp pistachios, finely chopped

TO DECORATE

a few rose petals (pale pink are good)
1 egg white, lightly beaten
caster sugar, for dipping
Pistachio pesto (see page 179)

Preheat the oven to 180°C/350°F/gas 4. Blitz the biscuits in a blender to make fine crumbs. Stir in the melted butter, then press the mix on to the bottom and up the sides of 6 holes of a deep muffin tray.

Beat the cream cheese and sugar together. Mix in the soured cream, then beat in the whole egg and the egg yolk. Stir in the rosewater and lemon juice. Spoon the cheese mixture into the muffin tins and sprinkle with the chopped pistachios. Bake for 10–12 minutes, or until just set. Chill in the muffin tray for 2 hours.

Meanwhile, prepare the decorations. Make some crystallised rose petals. Gently brush a few rose petals with the egg white, then dip in caster sugar. Carefully lay them on a plate and leave to dry. Make the pistachio pesto.

To serve, carefully run a knife around each cheesecake, ease them out and serve decorated with the crystallised rose petals and a drizzle of pistachio pesto.

another idea

- Instead of baking the cheesecakes in muffin tins, bake them in 6 x 10–12cm/4–5in round mini cake tins, until just set.

strawberry, nectarine and raspberry with amaretto sabayon

Another delicate, girly dessert! This one is very light and a slight step up from fruit salad. You can use a peach instead of a nectarine if you prefer.

SERVES 4
400g/13oz strawberries
1 nectarine, preferably white
150g/5oz raspberries

FOR THE SABAYON
4 egg yolks
25g/1oz caster sugar
25ml/1fl oz sweet white wine
1 tbsp amaretto liqueur

Hull and halve the strawberries. Stone the nectarine and cut into wedges. Leave the raspberries whole. Divide all the fruit between 4 serving bowls.

Put a saucepan of water on to boil. Put the egg yolks and sugar in a heatproof mixing bowl that fits neatly over the pan and whisk until white and frothy. Pour in the wine and amaretto and place the bowl on top of the saucepan. Whisk until the mixture is about 3 times its original bulk.

Spoon the sabayon over each portion of fruit, then glaze with a blow torch (or put under a hot grill) until golden on top. Serve immediately.

west country cider brandy syllabubs with cinnamon sugar shortbreads

Syllabub is a very traditional English dessert, very easy to make and surprisingly gorgeous. This one is a lovely Somerset version. The recipe makes quite a large quantity of shortbread (always better to have too much than too little, I find); if you have leftovers, the biscuits will keep in an airtight tin for a week or so, or you can freeze the dough and bake it freshly.

SERVES 6

3 tbsp Somerset cider brandy
125g/4oz caster sugar
¼ nutmeg, freshly grated
300ml/½ pint dry cider
800ml/1 pint 8fl oz double cream

FOR THE SHORTBREAD
300g/10oz plain flour
150g/5oz caster sugar
250g/8½oz butter

FOR THE CINNAMON SUGAR
25g/1oz caster sugar
¼ tsp ground cinnamon

Mix the cider brandy, sugar and nutmeg together in a bowl, so they are well combined. Pour in the dry cider and mix together.

Then, in a large bowl, whip the cream to soft peaks and gradually pour in the cider mixture, continuing to whisk as you do so. Pour the mixture into 6 wine glasses or sundae bowls and chill.

Now make the shortbread. It's easiest to do this in an electric mixer if you have one. Mix the flour and sugar together. Then cube the butter and add to the mixture. Using the dough hook, mix until well combined (with no lumps of butter left) and the dough starts to hold together. Do not over-mix.

Cut the ball in half. Roll out each piece between 2 pieces of silicone or parchment paper to a thickness of about 5mm/¼in. Place the pieces of dough on baking sheets or a board and chill in the fridge for about 30 minutes. (If you want to save some dough, wrap 1 piece in clingfilm and store it in the freezer. It will keep for 2–3 months and can be cut and baked from frozen.) Meanwhile, make the cinnamon sugar by combining the sugar and cinnamon together. Set aside.

Preheat the oven to 150°C/300°F/gas 2. Take the shortbread sheets out of the fridge and cut them into your desired biscuit shapes. I like long triangles, or, when I'm feeling romantic, little hearts (this all depends on whom I'm cooking for!). Lay the biscuits on 1 or 2 baking sheets. Bake for about 12–20 minutes, or until cooked but not golden – more sand-coloured. The timing will depend on the shape of your biscuits. Remove and sprinkle with the cinnamon sugar. Serve with the syllabubs.

low-fat hazelnut cake

Mum was a great savoury cook, but couldn't bake cakes to save her life. Except for this one, which was her *pièce de résistance* and always tasted great. Baking cakes was one of the first cooking skills I learnt, at the age of four, from my grandparents. This cake has little saturated fat (usually very high in cakes) as it contains no butter. It is also made with egg whites only, which are also low in fat and add a lightness to the cake.

SERVES 8

300g/10oz ground hazelnuts
300g/10oz caster sugar
8 egg whites
75g/3oz plain flour
raspberries, low-fat crème fraîche and icing
    sugar, to serve

Preheat the oven to 200°C/400°F/gas 6. Lightly oil the base of a deep 20cm/8in round springform cake tin and line with parchment or greaseproof paper. Blitz the ground nuts and sugar together in a food processor to mix well. Whisk the egg whites to soft peaks, then gently fold the nut mixture into the whites, then the flour.

Pour the mixture into the cake tin and bake for 35–40 minutes, until risen and pale golden on top. Serve with raspberries and low-fat crème fraîche and a dusting of icing sugar.

another idea

- Replace the hazelnuts with almonds or pistachios and mix in some fresh raspberries after the flour.

chocolate pots with peanut cookies

Mmmmmm…!! These incredibly rich little desserts look great served in espresso cups with the cookies resting on the saucer.

SERVES 6

FOR THE CHOCOLATE POTS

1 vanilla pod, split lengthways

300ml/½ pint double cream

125ml/4fl oz milk

300g/10oz good-quality dark chocolate,
   broken into pieces

3 egg yolks

50g/2oz icing sugar

FOR THE PEANUT COOKIES

75g/3oz butter, softened

50g/2oz crunchy peanut butter

50g/2oz caster sugar

50g/2oz light muscovado sugar

1 small egg, beaten

125g/4oz plain flour

½ tsp baking powder

pinch of salt

50g/2oz chopped peanuts

To make the chocolate pots, scrape the seeds from the vanilla pod into a saucepan, add the pod, the cream and milk and heat. Remove from the heat just before the mixture starts to boil, then stir in the chocolate pieces until smooth. Quickly beat in the egg yolks so that they don't start to cook. Pour the mixture into 6 individual dishes (ramekins or espresso cups are good) and chill until set.

To make the cookies, preheat the oven to 180°C/350°F/gas 4. Beat the butter and the peanut butter together, then beat in both the sugars, then the egg. Mix the flour, baking powder and salt together and fold into the peanut butter mixture, blending well. Gather the dough together to make a ball, then form it into a long sausage shape. Freeze or chill until hard. The recipe works best using frozen dough.

Slice the dough from frozen into 1cm/½ in-thick rounds, lay them slightly apart on baking sheets, and sprinkle on the chopped peanuts. Bake for about 15 minutes or until pale golden. Leave to cool and serve alongside the chocolate pots. The biscuits will keep for up to a week in an airtight tin.

crunchy rhubarb with orange fool

In this recipe the rhubarb is cooked very lightly, so it retains some crunch – a variation on the usual mushy version. The rhubarb base can also be used as a great partner for Greek yoghurt, panna cottas and even custard tarts. For the orange fool, I often use orange and mandarin oils from Sicily. These are great if you can get them; if not, just use the oranges.

SERVES 4

FOR THE RHUBARB BASE

2 pieces of stem ginger (from a jar of ginger in syrup)
4 sticks of young pink rhubarb
150g/5oz caster sugar

FOR THE ORANGE FOOL

300ml/½ pint double cream
3 tbsp icing sugar
finely grated zest and juice of 2 oranges
few drops of orange oil (optional)

First, make the rhubarb base. Cut the ginger into thin strips. Carefully slice the rhubarb into neat, very fine slices, about 3mm/⅛in thick. Set the ends aside.

Pour 200ml/7fl oz water into a saucepan and add the sugar. Bring slowly to the boil, stirring often until the sugar has dissolved. Add the rhubarb and ginger. Bring the mixture back to the boil, then immediately take it off the heat. Drain off the rhubarb and ginger in a sieve or colander, and pour the syrup back into the pan. Bring it back to the boil again and reduce by two-thirds. Add the rhubarb ends to the syrup while you are reducing it, as they will add colour. Lift them out with a slotted spoon when the the syrup has reduced. Stir in the rhubarb slices and ginger pieces. Set aside to cool.

For the orange fool, whip the cream with the sugar to make soft peaks. Fold in the orange zest and juice, and the orange oil, if using.

To assemble, spoon the rhubarb, ginger and syrup into the bottom of 4 large wine glasses. Top with the orange fool and leave to set in the fridge before serving.

elderflower and blackcurrant jellies

These are really pretty little jellies. Jelly is a great dessert as it is completely fat-free and this particular recipe is low in sugar as well. You can also experiment with different flavours. Champagne and peach are a lovely combination, or you can layer flavours like mango and lime... just have fun!

SERVES 6

4 sheets of leaf gelatine
800ml/1 pint 8fl oz sparkling elderflower pressé
225g/8oz mix of red, black and white currants, stripped from their stalks

Put the gelatine into a bowl, cover with cold water and set aside until softened. Gently heat 200ml/7fl oz of the elderflower pressé until it is hot. Lift the gelatine leaves from the water and squeeze out any excess liquid. Remove the elderflower pressé from the heat and stir in the gelatine leaves, continuing to stir until they are completely dissolved. Pour in the rest of the elderflower pressé.

Pour 1cm/½in of the elderflower liquid into the bottom of each of 6 glass dishes and divide the berries between them. Chill until set.

Pour the remaining jelly mix over the fruit and chill until completely set. Serve straight from the fridge.

spiced apricot and marzipan cake

This is a lighter take on the traditional fruit cake, which some people find too heavy. It's great for Easter, Christmas, or any celebration and is perfect for marzipan fans like me.

SERVES 8

225g/8oz butter, softened
225g/8oz caster sugar
4 eggs
225g/8oz self-raising flour
1 tsp ground cinnamon
50g/2oz almonds, chopped
50g/2oz pistachios, chopped
125g/4oz ready-to-eat dried apricots, chopped
100ml/3½fl oz milk
finely grated zest of 1 lemon
2 tbsp apricot jam
icing sugar, for dusting
about 350g/12oz marzipan (depending how
    thick you like it)
ribbon and mini chocolate or sugar-coated
    eggs, to decorate

Preheat the oven to 180°C/350°F/gas 4. Butter a deep 20cm/8in round cake tin and line with greaseproof paper. Beat the butter and sugar together until light and fluffy. Add the eggs one at a time, mixing well after each addition. Fold in the flour, cinnamon, nuts and apricots. Stir in the milk and lemon zest. Spoon the mixture into the cake tin and bake for 40–45 minutes, or until a skewer pushed into the centre comes out clean when removed. Leave in the tin to cool for 30 minutes, then turn the cake out, peel off the lining paper and leave to cool completely.

Put the jam in a small pan with 1 tablespoon water. Warm through, then use to brush over the top of the cake. On a work surface lightly dusted with icing sugar, roll out the marzipan to a 20cm/8in round. Gently lay the marzipan over the top of the cake and smooth down the surface with your hands. Trim the edges if necessary. Decorate with a pastel ribbon and mini eggs.

baked ginger plums

This very simple and healthy pudding somehow manages to leave you feeling refreshed, while still having a lovely, autumnal, comforting feel to it. It's delicious served with crème fraîche (the low-fat version if you like).

SERVES 4
8 deep red plums
50g/2oz stem ginger in syrup (from a jar),
    including 1 tbsp of syrup
crème fraîche, to serve (optional)

Preheat the oven to 180°C/350°F/gas 4. Halve and stone the plums and lay them on a baking sheet. Cut the ginger into thin strips and scatter over the plums. Drizzle the ginger syrup over and bake until the plums are soft and caramelised, about 15–20 minutes. Serve with crème fraîche if you like.

barbecued bananas

I can't tell you how great these actually are. The heat from the barbecue turns the fruit into a liquidy banana mush – brilliant served with vanilla ice cream and chocolate sauce.

Basically, you just place the whole bananas in their skins on to the barbie and leave them there for about 10 minutes, until they are dark black and starting to burst (but not charred).

the basics

I added this chapter to show you how to make some basic recipes, as they always come in handy. Some of these can be used as a starting point for more complex dishes. My basic tomato sauce, for example, provides a great base for soup, stews and casseroles. Other recipes, like the pestos, marinades and stocks, can be made and stored (either in the fridge or freezer). You can then use them to rustle up a quick and tasty dinner whenever you like. I also wanted to explain in simple terms how to tackle some more 'difficult' ingredients. Wrestling with lobsters, artichokes and oysters can seem quite daunting to the amateur cook or even trainee chef, if I remember rightly! I hope that my instructions will conquer any qualms…

basic tomato sauce

This sauce is fantastic used over wholemeal pasta, or as a base for casseroles. If you add some diced pancetta at the beginning, then some stock to make a soupy consistency, a little basil and some crème fraîche, it makes an excellent soup. Just experiment!

MAKES ENOUGH FOR 4 SERVINGS
2 tbsp olive oil
1 onion, finely chopped
3 garlic cloves, finely chopped
splash of white wine
400g/13oz can chopped tomatoes
2 pinches of dried oregano
1 pinch of dried chilli flakes
salt and freshly ground black pepper
small pinch of sugar
handful of chopped fresh basil

Heat the oil in a saucepan and fry the onion and garlic until softened but not brown. Add the white wine and let it bubble for a minute or two, to cook off the alcohol.

Stir in the tomatoes, oregano and chilli, then cover and cook slowly for about 30 minutes, until thickened to a sauce. Season to taste with salt, pepper and sugar. Scatter in the basil, and serve.

basil pesto

I love pesto so much. It has an amazing aroma, is bursting with flavours and can be used for so many more dishes than just pasta. Stir it into roasted vegetables, stuff chicken with pesto and mozzarella, or mix it into mayonnaise or cream cheese...the list is endless! You can also make your own variations by adding chillies, sun-dried tomatoes or olives. Pesto is best made with a pestle and mortar, which squeezes the aromatic juices out of the basil. If you're short of time, however, use an electric blender. This pesto will beat shop-bought by miles.

MAKES 1 BATCH
125g/4oz roasted pine nuts
½ garlic clove
1 large bunch of basil
200ml/7fl oz good-quality olive oil
about 125g/4oz Parmesan cheese, cut into small chunks

Put the pine nuts, garlic, basil and 3 tablespoons of the oil in a blender or food processor and blitz down – not too fine, though, as you still want a bit of texture. Add the Parmesan and continue blitzing, drizzling in the rest of olive oil bit by bit. Taste as you add the oil and stop when you've achieved your preferred flavour and consistency. The pesto will keep in the fridge for up to 2 weeks, as long as the surface is covered with olive oil.

pistachio pesto

Okay, so I admit this isn't really a pesto, but it does look quite like one. It also tastes yummy with ice-cream or sorbet.

MAKES ENOUGH FOR 4 SERVINGS
150g/5oz pistachios
125g/4oz caster sugar
squeeze of lemon juice

Blitz the pistachios in a blender or food processor until semi-coarse/fine, then tip them into a bowl.

Pour 100ml/3½fl oz water into a saucepan and add the sugar. Bring to the boil over a low heat, stirring, until the sugar has dissolved. Turn up the heat and boil to reduce slightly to a thin sugar syrup. You should have about 150ml/¼ pint.

Gradually pour the syrup into the ground pistachios to make a semi-wet consistency. Squeeze in a little lemon juice, and serve.

chicken stock

This is a basic chicken stock recipe. You can make it with raw chicken pieces (thighs, drumsticks, wings) or carcasses, or both. You can even use the leftover carcass from your roast chicken dinner. In professional kitchens the chicken is always roasted before boiling for stock, but I find it's perfectly fine to make the stock from raw chicken. This recipe makes a large quantity, as I like to have loads of stock handy in the freezer, but it's an easy recipe to scale down if you want to make less. You can also reduce the finished stock down to make a superb soup.

MAKES ABOUT 3.5 LITRES/NEARLY 6 PINTS STOCK

about 1.5kg/3lb 5oz cooked or raw chicken carcasses (or chicken pieces)
2 onions
3 carrots
4 celery sticks
2 leeks
3 garlic cloves, kept whole
4 parsley sprigs
2 thyme sprigs
2 rosemary sprigs
2 bay leaves
4 whole peppercorns

Place the chicken into a very large pot – big enough to take the veg. and water as well. Roughly chop all the vegetables, add them to the pan with the rest of the ingredients and pour in about 6 litres/10½ pints water – enough just to cover the carcasses. Bring to the boil, skim off any froth and fat with a ladle, then lower the heat and simmer for 3–4 hours. Skim off and discard any froth and fat from time to time as it comes to the surface.

Drain off and reserve the stock. Allow it to cool, then pass the liquid through a sieve to remove any remaining bits and pieces. Pour the stock into storage containers. It will keep for 2–3 days in the fridge or can be frozen for 2–3 months.

another idea

• If you want to make a Thai-flavoured chicken stock base, substitute the herbs in the basic recipe with 3 lemongrass stalks, 4 kaffir lime leaves, 1 piece of roughly chopped fresh root ginger, a piece of galangal and a bunch of chopped coriander. Finish with a good squeeze of lemon juice.

fish stock

I've included this recipe as it's great to have a
good fish stock base at hand for a number of the
dishes in this book. There are some decent ready-
made fish stocks available, but home-made is
unbeatable.

MAKES ABOUT 2 LITRES/3½ PINTS
  1.5kg/3lb 5oz fish bones
  2 celery sticks
  ½ fennel bulb
  1 onion
  1 small leek
  1 plump garlic clove
  2 tbsp olive oil
  125ml/4fl oz white wine
  4 parsley sprigs
  1 bay leaf
  1 thyme sprig

Wash the fish bones thoroughly and remove any
'extras' such as eye-balls or gills. Roughly chop
the fish bones, all the vegetables and the garlic.

Heat the olive oil in a large saucepan and fry the
vegetables until softened but not golden. Add the
fish bones and continue to fry for 4–5 minutes,
stirring occasionally. Pour in the white wine and
simmer to reduce the liquid by a third.

Add 3 litres/5¼ pints water and the herbs.
Bring the mixture to the boil, skim off any froth
or fat and reduce the heat to a simmer. Simmer
for 20 minutes only, then drain off and reserve
the liquid. (Make sure you don't cook the stock
for any longer, or it will turn bitter.)

You can now reduce the stock for a more concen-
trated flavour, or cool it and store it in the fridge
where it will keep for 2–3 days. It can also be
frozen in manageable batches for 1–2 months.

healthy marinades

These two delicious but healthy marinades can be used to liven up fish, chicken and lamb. Great for barbecues, they can also be used for grilling and roasting.

thai

This is excellent for grilled chicken or fish.

MAKES ENOUGH FOR APPROX. 2 CHICKEN
    BREASTS
2 lemongrass stalks
1 lime
2.5cm/1in piece of fresh root ginger
1 red chilli, deseeded and chopped
2 cloves garlic, finely chopped
3 kaffir lime leaves
1 tbsp chopped coriander
1 tsp soy sauce
1 tbsp vegetable oil
salt and freshly ground black pepper

Chop the lemongrass into small pieces. Juice the lime and finely grate the zest. Peel and grate the ginger. Mix all the ingredients together in a small bowl. Pour the marinade over fish or chicken, ensuring that each piece is well-coated. Allow to marinate for 30 minutes before grilling or barbecuing.

mediterranean

This marinade has a lovely herby flavour with a touch of bite from the chilli and lemon. It's fantastic for lamb or roasted vegetables.

MAKES ENOUGH FOR 3 LAMB STEAKS
1 tbsp lemon juice
3 cloves garlic, finely chopped
pinch of dried chilli flakes
1 tsp chopped rosemary
1 tsp chopped parsley
2 tbsp olive oil
salt and freshly ground black pepper

Mix all the ingredients in a small bowl, then brush on to your lamb or vegetables. Leave to marinate for 2 hours before roasting or barbecuing.

flavoured oils

Flavoured oils are incredibly easy to make and are great for pepping up dressings and other dishes. Always start with good-quality olive oil. Stored in a cool, dark place, they should keep for 3–4 weeks.

chilli oil

This is a really versatile oil which will liven up your soups and pastas. I like it drizzled in minestrone soup or added to Thai chicken stock (see page 180).

MAKES 500ML/17FL OZ
8 dried chillies
1 tsp dried chilli flakes
1 rosemary sprig
500ml/17fl oz extra-virgin olive oil

Put the chillies, chilli flakes and rosemary in a sterilised bottle, pour in the olive oil and leave to infuse for 2 weeks in a cool, dark place before using, shaking the bottle occasionally. Remove the rosemary before using.

ginger and orange oil

This is a good oil for using in salad dressings and stir-fries. It also makes the perfect finish for a watercress and orange salad and is wonderful drizzled over roasted duck.

MAKES 500ML/17FL OZ
½ tsp coriander seeds
1 orange
5cm/2in piece of fresh root ginger
500ml/17fl oz light olive oil

Heat a small, dry pan, then add the coriander seeds and fry them briefly until they just start to colour – this brings out their flavour. Leave to cool. Using a potato peeler, peel the zest from the orange in large strips, being careful not to take off too much white pith as this will make the oil bitter.

Cut the ginger into thin matchsticks. Put the coriander seeds, orange zest and ginger in a sterilised bottle, pour in the olive oil and leave to infuse for 3 days in a cool, dark place. Strain before using.

garlicky herb oil

A good basic stand-by which adds flavour to fish, meat, dressings, pasta – you name it! It's much better than garlic butter, and healthier too.

MAKES 500ML/17FL OZ
3 garlic cloves, lightly bashed
2 rosemary sprigs
2 thyme sprigs
½ tsp black peppercorns
3 bay leaves
500ml/17fl oz extra-virgin olive oil

Put all the first 5 ingredients into a sterilised bottle, then pour in the oil. Leave to infuse for 1 week in a cool, dark place. Strain before using.

flavoured salts

These flavoured salts are great to use as a basic seasoning and can be sprinkled on to meat, fish and vegetables before cooking. The seaweed salt is based on a traditional Japanese recipe and is delicious on salads or sprinkled on soups or sushi. The salts can be stored in a jar until needed, so it's worth making a large batch.

spiced paprika salt

This makes a wonderfully spicy salt, and it is especially good rubbed on to chicken pieces and squash before roasting.

MAKES 1 BATCH
125g/4oz sea salt
1 tsp smoked paprika
½ tsp garlic powder
½ tsp dried oregano
½ tsp ground coriander
½ tsp ground cumin
½ tsp curry powder

Mix all the ingredients together in a small bowl and go forth and spice things! The salt can be stored in a sterilised jar with a tight-fitting lid.

seaweed salt

Good for seasoning miso soup, sushi rolls and soba noodle dishes.

MAKES ABOUT 225G/8OZ
3 sheets of nori seaweed
1 tsp sesame seeds
1 tsp wasabi powder
225g/8oz sea salt crystals

Place the seaweed on a baking sheet and lightly toast it under a medium grill until it changes colour, but does not burn. Heat a dry pan, add the sesame seeds and cook until they are lightly toasted and golden, tossing the pan occasionally so that they don't burn.

In an electric blender, blitz the seaweed, wasabi and salt together, then mix in the sesame seeds. Store in a sterilised jar with a tight-fitting lid.

flavoured butters

These butters should be used only in moderation as they're high in saturated fat. But as I've already said, this sort of fat is a lesser enemy of a healthy body than sugar and processed foods or hydrogenated fats. If you make up a good amount, you can shape the flavoured butter into a log, wrap and freeze it, ready for slicing off whenever you need some.

garlic and chilli butter

This yummy butter is great for livening up steamed vegetables. Allow it to melt over the veg.

MAKES ABOUT 250G/8½OZ
250g/8½oz butter, softened
2 garlic cloves, crushed
½ tsp dried chilli flakes

Beat the butter until smooth, then beat in the garlic and chilli. Roll it into a sausage shape, wrap in greaseproof paper, then foil, and freeze. It will keep for up to 2–3 months.

thai-flavoured butter

This butter is great melted over chicken, prawns and fish. It's not very authentic, but who cares when it tastes this good?

MAKES ABOUT 250G/8½OZ
250g/8½oz butter, softened
½ lemongrass stalk (base only)
1 tsp chopped fresh root ginger
1 garlic clove, crushed
½ red chilli, deseeded and finely chopped
1 tbsp chopped coriander

Beat the butter until smooth. Finely chop the lemongrass and mix it into the butter with the rest of the ingredients. Roll the butter into a sausage shape and store as for Garlic and chilli butter (see left).

anchovy and lemon butter

Anchovies lend a fantastic, savoury flavour and people are always surprised that this butter isn't too fishy. It tastes great with steamed vegetables, artichokes and grilled meats.

MAKES ABOUT 250G/8½OZ
250g/8½oz unsalted butter, softened
8–10 salted anchovy fillets
juice of 1 lemon
freshly ground black pepper

Beat the butter until smooth. Finely chop the anchovies and beat them into the butter, then beat in the lemon juice. Add a grinding of pepper and store as for Garlic and chilli butter (see left).

how to cook a lobster

In some of my recipes I've specified using cooked lobster. I did this because they're easier to buy in the high street. But if you can find live lobsters, so much the better – mainly because you can guarantee how fresh they are. I also think that it's good to be in touch with what your food really is. It's all too easy to forget and appreciate that a lobster is a live sea-creature, that a steak comes from a cow and that your chicken tikka once had wings...so it's back to basics.

in the pot

The most humane way to kill a lobster is to freeze it first. This will put it to sleep – far easier than chasing it round the kitchen! Stroking them between the eyes also has the same effect, but watch out for those claws...

Place the live lobster(s) in the freezer for about 2 hours. Bring a pan of water to the boil – allow 3 litres/5¼ pints per 600g–1kg/1lb 5oz–2lb lobster – and add the lobster. If cooking more than one, don't overcrowd the pan. Cover with a lid and boil for about 3 minutes per 500g/1lb. This is long enough to parboil the lobster, which can then be used and cooked further in other dishes. If you want to cook the lobster completely (for example, if using for a salad), allow 4 minutes per 500g/1lb. The lobster will have turned red. Remove the lobster from the water and use accordingly.

roasting and grilling

If you are going to grill or roast your lobster rather than boiling it, you will have to be a bit braver with your preparation. The following method may seem a bit gruesome, but it is quick and effective.

Place the lobster on a secure chopping board. Pull the tail out flat. The idea is to split the lobster from head to tail down its midline, cutting through the nerve centres that run down its back to kill it instantly.

Take a large, very sharp chef's knife. Find the cross-hatch behind the lobster's head, plunge the tip of the knife right down, piercing it behind the head, then bring the rest of the knife down and through the back and tail, cutting the lobster in half. Then cut through the front of the head.

You can now place the lobster on a tray and grill or roast it accordingly.

how to open oysters

I've said it before, but I love oysters! They taste of the sea and make me very happy. It's important to open and serve them properly – treat them with respect, be gentle and avoid damaging the flesh. I recommend serving 6 oysters per person as a starter or 3 per person for canapés.

Opening oysters can be awkward, but you'll soon get the hang of it. You will need an oyster knife, or a knife with a strong, stainless-steel blade. First, take a clean cloth and wrap it around your hand (if the knife slips, your hand will be covered). Now sandwich the oyster between the cloth and a work surface.

Place the point of your knife in the hinge of the shell and gently work it in. As you start to get more space in between the shells, start twisting until the hinge gives and you hear a crack. The oyster should now open easily. Pick out any bits of shell. Then loosen the main muscle. Serve in their shells on crushed ice with lemon wedges, a dash of Tabasco and a splash of Shallot vinegar (see below).

shallot vinegar
1 banana shallot, finely chopped
300ml/½ pint good-quality red wine vinegar

Mix the ingredients together and serve with your oysters.

sophie's foolproof eggs

poached eggs
Everyone poaches eggs differently, but this is my method which always produces pretty perfect ones. I recommend that you poach only 3 at a time and use a large saucepan.

> **200ml/7fl oz white wine vinegar**
> **3 fresh free-range eggs**

Put 3 litres/5¼ pints water and the vinegar into a large saucepan and start bringing it to the boil. You want to catch it when there are just fine, champagne-like bubbles rising, and before any large bubbles start appearing. At this point, crack the eggs one at a time into the water, trying to keep the break clean and as close to the water's surface as possible. Be gentle!

You can now bring the water up to a steady boil and cook for about 2–3 minutes. If serving straight away, scoop each egg out with a slotted spoon and serve. If making a big batch to serve later, scoop out the eggs and put into cold water. When needed, reheat for a few seconds, in a small pan of boiling water.

boiled eggs
The best way to boil eggs is to start with cold water, as this causes less cracks and breakages. So put your eggs in a saucepan and cover with cold water. Bring to the boil, then simmer for 3–4 minutes for soft-boiled, or 10–12 minutes for hard-boiled.

drinks

You really must drink at least 1.5 litres/2½ pints of water a day. It helps weight loss and maintains good skin condition and body function. You'll also find you have a lot more energy and feel clearer-headed. But drinking just tap water when you're following a low-sugar eating plan can get quite boring. Sometimes you want something a bit more exciting on the taste buds. Many bought fruit juices and branded drinks contain masses of sugar, so I've included a few non-alcoholic low-sugar alternatives.

alcoholic drinks

There are times when you're going to want an alcoholic drink. The following are probably among the more healthy, low-calorie drinks you can have:

- Vodka, lime and soda. Use fresh lime juice, not cordial as it contains sugar

- Gin and slimline tonic

- White wine spritzer (white wine is quite high in sugar)

- Rum and Diet Coke...not ideal, so limit yourself to one, as Coke is full of nasties!

raspberry and mint crush

This is summer in a glass. The perfect accompaniment to a picnic in the sun.

SERVES 4
3 mint sprigs
225g/8oz raspberries
juice of ½ lemon
2 tbsp Splenda sweetener
750ml/1¼ pints carbonated water
ice cubes, to serve

Pick the mint leaves off the stems and tear them into a bowl. Crush the raspberries, mint, lemon juice and sweetener together with a fork. Add the carbonated water and some ice cubes. Stir and serve.

ginger–lemon zinger

A real tongue-tingler, this is deliciously fresh-tasting and zesty.

SERVES 4
5cm/2in piece of fresh root ginger
juice of 5 lemons
4 tbsp Splenda sweetener
750ml/1¼ pints carbonated water
ice cubes, to serve

Peel the ginger and slice thinly. Place the ginger, lemon juice and sweetener in a saucepan over a medium heat. Bring to the boil, then remove from the heat. Allow to cool and infuse. Place a few ice cubes in each glass. Mix the ginger mixture with the water and serve over the ice.

mint and lime crush

A little something to transport you to a desert island, this is kinda like a mojito without the rum.

SERVES 4
4 mint sprigs
5 limes
Splenda sweetener, to taste
couple of handfuls of ice cubes
750ml/1¼ pints carbonated water

Pick the mint leaves off the stems and divide the leaves between 4 glasses. Cut the limes into wedges and put 1¼ limes in each glass. Add sweetener to taste. Crush the ice with a rolling pin and divide between the glasses. Top with the fizzy water and serve.

index